RELATIONSHIP COMMUNICATION

THE THINGS THAT ARE TRULY IMPORTANT

The Essential Relationship Workbook To Build Strong Connections With Your Partner

Kian Lloyd

Copyright © 2020 Kian Lloyd

All Rights Reserved

Table of Contents

PART 1	9
Chapter 1	10
Before We Begin	10
Possible Causes	22
Chapter 2	32
Secret Tips 1-2	32
Step One-Talking to Yourself	32
SCENARIO	33
Step Two- Have a Few Ice Breakers	36
Good Ice Breakers	37
Bad Ice Breakers	39
How These Tips Help	40
Chapter 3	42
Secret Tips 3-4	42
Tip Three- Self Disclosure	43
Tip Four- Engage the Other Person Fully	50
How to Engage Them	53
How These Tips Help	55
Chapter 4	57
Secret Tips 5-6	57
Tip Five- Etiquette During a Convo	57
Tip Six- Etiquette When Leaving a Conversation	65

How These Tips Help 69

Chapter 5 70

Secret Tips 7-10 70

Tip Seven- Get Out of Your Head 70

Tip Eight- Boost Your Self Esteem 72

Tip Nine- Handle Rejection with Pride 73

Tip Ten- Don't Latch On 75

How These Tips Help 75

Chapter 6 77

Bonus Tips 77

How to know if it is more than just being shy 78

introduction 79

Reignite your relationship 79

Chapter 1 100

How Technology Has Affected Our Communication Skills 100

Possible Causes 106

Chapter 2 115

Conversation Tips 115

Step One-Talking to Yourself 115

SCENARIO 116

Step Two- Have a Few Ice Breakers 119

Real Ice Breakers 120

Bad Ice Breakers 122

How These Tips Help 123

Chapter 3 125

Holding a Conversation 125

Tip Three- Self Disclosure 126

Tip Four- Engage the Other Person Fully 133

How to Engage Them 136

How These Tips Help 138

Getting Through a Conversation 139

Tip Five- Etiquette During a Conversation 139

Tip Six- Etiquette When Leaving a Conversation 147

How These Tips Help 150

Chapter 5 151

Additional Tips 151

Tip Seven- Get Out of Your Head 152

Tip Eight- Boost Your Self Esteem 153

Tip Nine- Handle Rejection with Pride 155

Tip Ten- Don't Latch On 156

How These Tips Help 156

Chapter 6 158

After the Tips 158

How to know if it is more than just being shy 159

CHAPTER 1 162

five keys to fire up 162

Why Is There No Fire in Your Relationship? 163

The Five Keys to Reignite the Fire in Your Relationship 167

Key #1: Making a Game-Time Decision 167

Key #2: Know & Share Your Turn-ons 167

Key #3: Maintain the Mystery 168

Key #4: Change It Up 168

Key #5: Connecting On All Sexual Cylinders 168

Medical Reasons for a Decrease in Sexual Desire 169

Things You Can Do to Improve Your Sex Drive 171

CHAPTER 2 174

Secret key #1 174

Making a game-time decision 174

Prepare for that Game-time Move 175

Uncertainty 176

Complexity 177

Consequences 177

Reasonably Predict the Outcome 178

Plan Your Approach 179

Set the Scene 180

Explore Together 181

Create A Vision 182

CHAPTER 3 187

SECRET KEY #2 187

KNOW AND SHARE YOUR TURN-ONS 187

Ten Things Women Do That Make Men Hot 188

Ten Things Men Do That Make Women Hot 193

CHAPTER 4 200

SECRET KEY #3 200

MAINTAIN THE MYSTERY 200

Give Cause to Question 202

Don't Always Be Readily Available 204

Don't Talk Too Much 205

Some Things Are Better Left to the Imagination 206

Challenge Your Partner 207

Let Your Partner Earn Your Compliments 208

Encourage Silent Communication 209

Create the Mystery 210

CHAPTER 5 213

SECRET KEY #4 213

CHANGE IT UP 213

Tools and Toys 217

CHAPTER 6 222

SECRET KEY #5 222

CONNECTING ON 222

Hot Sex Can Change Your Professional Prowess 223

Hot Sex Makes You More Attractive 225

You'll Identify with Your Newly Discovered Sexuality 226

PART V 230

Make Him Feel Safe 251

Respect and Compassion 257

Be Confident 267

Give and Take on the Lead 274

Open, Honest, Consistent Communication 284

Equality and Respect 295

Acceptance for Who They Are 301

Special Bonus Tips 313

PART 1

Chapter 1

Before We Begin

Before we jump right into the secret steps, there is some basic information that you should know. This will help you to better understand the basis of your communication block. In truth this world is a lot different than it used to be back in the days of covered wagons and community bathing, but maybe, it isn't better in some ways. Yes, now we have technology and indoor plumbing, but there is a haze over us that maybe is not as friendly as it used to be.

People call this the age of communication, based on the ease in which we can talk to people miles away from us. That is a great thing in all, but how about the people that are right next to us? Over seventy percent of the world's population admits to having a problem with communicating properly with people in their own families, and they definitely can't hold a proper conversation with strangers or basic acquaintances.

This is a problem, but is it really so different than the days of yore? Let us compare, shall we?

In the old days (before telephones were in every household, even before the invention of the telephone) it was so much easier to talk to people face to face. That is because for the longest time, it was the only form of communication, other than the post that came every week, or the occasional messenger pigeon that often took days to reach a destination seventy miles away. If you wanted to have a full on conversation in real time with someone, you had to go to their house, and talk to them. This meant that communication was futile to survival, because if you needed something you had to ask for it. You would have to communicate regularly with everyone around you. Walking down the street, it was customary to greet everyone with a smile, and a "hello, how are you today?" To not do so was considered bad manners.

Humans had to interact by speaking several times a day, and as a result, everyone was more friendly to each other, because you never know when you might need their help. People regularly dropped by their friends' houses unannounced and unplanned, because they had no way to call ahead to see if they were available. These visitors were not turned away, they were greeted with open arms. Children came in to greet the guests, before being sent back outside to play, unless the visitor wished to speak with them as well. Often, these visitors were asked to join the family for a meal before heading back out into their travels. During these meals, stories were swapped, and laughter filled the air. As the visitor left, they were followed by a chorus to come again any time, and they echoed by extending their own invitation to those they visited.

Children were taught from a young age how to socialize. They were sent outside to make their own friends, and taught how to be self sufficient. This gave them the confidence to speak to others. In school, they were instructed on what was appropriate conversation, and what was not. Children were often taught not to speak unless spoken to. This was to teach them not to interrupt those that were talking, and to truly listen to those around them. They were not taught to listen to make a reply, but were taught to listen so they could learn. This made them become friendly, and compassionate adults that were able to hold efficient conversation in the highest of social settings. Even home schooled children were taught how to behave when company was over, and were taught social cues by their parents. This was important, because even the most basic of farmers were visited often by the mayor of the town, or the pastor, and if the family, or even the children did not know how to socialize, it was an embarrassment. Of course, people were understanding, but conversation was key to survival, and if you were not good at communicating, it could sometimes be hard for someone to understand you, and children were taught this so they would take their social lessons seriously.

Strangers were welcomed with open arms as well. There was not a stigma that strangers were a bad thing, as you couldn't make friends if you weren't nice to strangers. Talking to even the oddest of strangers was a breeze. If a new person rode into town, they were welcomed into the home by the mayor or local pastor depending on the jurisdiction of the town. Sometimes even the sheriff invited the stranger over to his house. They person was treated like family, and served a fine feast to replenish their energy from their long journey, and that dinner was spent conversing about life, and getting to know this stranger. By the end of the evening, generally the house was filled with laughter as stories were swapped like they had been friends since birth. Strangers were not made to feel uncomfortable, or like an outsider. If the stranger had a trade, they were sent on to the local person who was an expert on the trade for an internship or to help and expand the knowledge about the subject. If there was no one who was an expert in that trade, this person was set up with help to start it up if they planned to stay in town long. Drifters were even more highly revered, as they had so many stories of different places they had been, and often he would spend his time in the town at various houses as he told his tales over and over again, entertaining the locals, and getting room and board and food for doing nothing more than telling stories of the places he had been.

People gathered together all of the time. Most weekends were filled with gatherings of friends and family, and even some nights during the week there were people gathering together for fun and festivity. Women regularly gathered in what were called knitting circles, where they would swap project and techniques, and have tea. They chatted about their weeks as they knitted, crocheted or stitched together. Young ladies were brought up in these environments as well, and they learned not only valuable skills, but how to speak and act like ladies. When in a social setting, the ladies were very eloquent, and well made up. Every social setting was a reason to look their best, and they made sure that they did.

Acquaintances that met on the street would stop and chat with each other. Even if they were in a hurry, they were never in too much of a hurry to stop and say a quick hello, and extend an invitation to stop by the house sometime. This way of life made even people you didn't know that well feel like family. You treated everyone with the respect you wish you received, and in return that respect was bestowed upon you.

Communicating with your neighbors, and inviting people into your home meant that they would be more willing to do the same for you. Even acquaintances were often seen mingling together, just like the best of friends.

People that did not live in town were no less social, as they still had to make regular trips into town to buy the necessities they could not make themselves. These trips were treated as an all day event. The night before they were to set off into town, they bathed and went to bed earlier than usual. Then they were up before the sun the next day and they hitched up the horses to the wagon and headed into town wearing their best clothes. Once in town, they visited the store first, to ensure that they had what they needed. They only picked up the textiles they needed to make the things they needed at home, and since they had no refrigeration in that time period, they did not have to worry about anything spoiling. If there was any money left over, the children would be allowed to buy some candy, often having to share, but since a penny would fill a bag, there was not much worry about anyone feeling left out. Often, if the family didn't have money to get their kids some candy, and the shopkeeper knew they were from the rural areas, he would give the children a few pieces free of charge. The children would then thank the shopkeeper with a sincere gratitude, and savor their candies, often making them stretch for several days. After their store visit, they would go to visit some friends and family that lived in town. They often would be invited for meals at various people's homes. Back then it was considered very rude to not offer a meal to a visitor, and it was even more rude to turn down a meal without a valid reason. However, even if you just ate at someone else's house, you would be fed a light snack at the current place you were at. Famine was considered the only excuse not to eat at someone's house as you would not want to deplete someone else's rations.

After a supper at their last stop for the day in town, the adults would chat as the children played, and got well worn out. This was one of the few times that children could stay up with the adults, and were allowed to be outside well after dark. If it was a nice night, often the adults would gather out under the stars and watch the children frolic about and enjoy the evening. Finally, well after sun down, they family would pack back into the wagon, and head home. After unloading their items from the store, they would head to bed, anxiously anticipating the next time they could make a trip into town. The children would go to sleep dreaming about the day's events, and the adults would sleep well, thoroughly exhausted from the adventure they had that day.

As crazy as this all seems, if you read any Laura Ingalls Wilder book, you will find these events to be true. Life was a simpler time then in some ways. Though there was more work to be done, it was easier to enjoy it knowing that you could look forward to something every day, and never knowing when a visitor was going to stop by put mystery in every single day.

So what happened? It seems like things today have made a complete one hundred and eighty degree turn from where things used to be. We are going in the opposite direction from where we used to be, and yet we claim that it is all for peace and acceptance. People are so closed off, and they never really talk to anyone. That is the saddest thing to see in all honesty.

Take a walk outside. How many people would you see? One? Two? Or would you even see any? Once upon a time, the whole block would be alight with people out chatting. Now it is always almost dead. People stay inside, and hide behind their fancy screens, and their technology. Children rarely go outdoors, unless they have old fashioned parents.

The media portrays the darkness of the world, filled with violence and fear. Children are shooting up schools rather than making friends. That is majorly contributed to by the fact that bullies are everywhere. The neighborly friends with anyone vibe has completely disappeared. If anyone drops by someone's house unannounced, they are met with the double barrel of a shot gun aimed at their face, rather than welcomed inside. Trips into town are hurried, as people just want to get the necessities and head back home to sit in front of the television. No one drops by friend's houses any more. If it can be avoided, they don't even leave the house. A lot of people now just order what they need and have it delivered overnight to their house. You can even do your grocery shopping this way.

Friendships have changed as well. It used to be if you saw your friend in the street, you greeted them with enthusiasm. Now it seems people hide from those that they know to avoid having to spend prolonged time in public. This causes those that they know to feel offended, yet simultaneously relieved, then abhorred that they feel relieved, so they take it out on the person who avoided them, and that is how anger and resentment breeds.

Dinner invitations are very rare, even when people have company over. The company is ushered out before a meal happens, so people can avoid having to offer a meal to their company. Rare dinner invitations are planned out weeks in advance, and often canceled last minute. No one sits around the table and shares stories anymore, unless it is a holiday that they have to attend. Children are not even sent outside to play with the neighborhood kids. They have strict play dates set up, and are not allowed outside unless they are supervised inside a fenced in yard.

Children are not taught how to be civilized in public either. All manners classes have been removed from schools, and are rarely taught at home. Children do not get to spend time learning how to behave, and how to hold a proper conversation in every day life. This leads to them growing up unsure of how to approach people. This causes a great dip in respect for others. It is only getting worse.

Drifters are now treated like lepers. People no longer sit in awe of their wondrous stories, instead, they are treated like dirt. This is because people can just do a quick search on the internet about all the places this person has been, and rather than listen to a human tell the tale, they would rather read about it from the web. That way they don't have to waste their food and space on some stranger. This aloof way that they are treated has lead to a stigma that homeless people are horrible, and that is the farthest from the truth.

Go down any New York street, and you will see people hustling and bustling about, and thousands of people pressed together, but they never acknowledge each other, unless it is to say something rude. They all have frowns on their faces, and rarely look up from their phones, or whatever it may be that they are doing. A person that waves is laughed at or scorned. There are so many people, and it is so full of hate, and rudeness, that it is better to just keep your mouth shut and stay inside.

The world has become a silent, sullen place. With how angry it has become it is no wonder why so many people have trouble talking with others. So do not feel alone, the entire world seems to have some semblance of a problem with communication, which makes it even harder for those with social anxiety or extreme shyness to talk to anyone that they do not know extremely well.

Possible Causes

There are many possible causes for this silence struck pandemic. Most of it can be attributed to one or more of the many technological advances that we have seen over the years. No one person has been able to pinpoint exactly what it is that has changed the amicable ways of the world. Here are some of the possible causes, and you can try to decide for yourself what you think has been the downfall of communication.

The Telephone: The invention of the telephone made it easier to take the human element out of a conversation. Instead of going to someone's house every so often and staying a few hours, and having a meal, they could call to say what needed to be said, and then cut the conversation short with the excuse that they were wracking up too many minutes that month. They didn't have to stay on the phone yacking for hours on end, because generally, the person on the other end of the line agreed and hung up as well.

The telephone, back when it was invented, was so expensive that only the rich people, and government agencies owned them. Invented in nineteen eighty nine by Alexander Graham-Bell, it was the most technologically advanced thing since the dawn of electricity. In the beginning, it cost over a thousand dollars to own a single phone. To make a call, Bell Telephone Industries charged a dollar a minute to dispatch that call. That was a lot of money considering the average worker was lucky to make fifty cents an hour. One minute call time would have been two hours wages, so most average wage households did not have a telephone in the house. That was until the mid nineteen hundreds, after Henry Ford invented the concept of mass production. A company made a telephone that was way cheaper than Bell Industries ancient phone design, and they found a better way to dispatch calls to make the calls cheaper. During this time, wages went up a lot as well. By this time the minimum wage was about two dollars an hour. This made phones more common in average households. By the nineteen seventies, a home phone was a staple in each household, and calls only cost ten cents a minute. This was a great thing, as by this time, wages were up to seven dollars an hour for minimum wage. The company that was instrumental in lowering the price of the phone? Well it is known today as AT&T.

Due to its cost, the telephone may not have been the downfall of modern communication, but it definitely could have had a hand in it. Especially as it became easier, and cheaper to purchase. People called rather than stopped by, and these calls did not have to drone on and on, as time was money. This allowed conversation to become shorter, and it made its way into everyday life as well.

Television: The television was a lot cheaper than the telephone was. It was also a way to get the news a lot easier, as you didn't have to wait until a friend heard something and get back to you. There were also some good programs to watch during the day that entertained people. This entertainment made them want to stay inside, and watch it all day. Well the adults at least. Children were still sent outside to play.

The original television was black and white and only had three channels. It was small, and could sit on the dining room table. Brand new, they cost about three hundred dollars, and they had really long rabbit ear antennas. At the beginning, this was the only option you had, but as time went on, there were bigger console televisions available. Eventually, the color television was introduced, and some time after that, more channels were added, as cable became a thing. More and more time was spent inside watching TV. Not just by adults anymore, either. Children were inside more often and watched shows that were geared towards their age groups. People went out and mingled with their neighbors less and less.

Television alone probably was not the downfall of the communication era, but it was a precedent to it. A lot of people began staying inside to watch their soaps instead of going outside to spend time with actual people. For the longest time, children were still sent out to play while the parents watched TV, but as the parents moved to colored cable, the children got the still working black and white rabbit eared television, and the trend progressed as in the older days, television sets lasted forever.

Game Consoles: Today there are several hi-tech game consoles out ther for people to choose from, and they are often played for hours on end, while the player ignores the outside world. Back when they were first invented, they were a lot different, but no less desirable. They were the envy of every household, and a child that had one was instantly popular, but he never used that popularity because he was too busy inside playing his new game. When the original Atari came out, it was the sensation that swept the nation.

The first ever game console was nothing like the ones we have today. They took a lot more effort to play. To make a single move, you had to write a program first. This was difficult, but the kids in those days didn't mind, as to them it was a game console, and that was the coolest thing they had ever seen. They also learned about computer programming before home computers were a thing. As time progressed, the programs were written into the game at production, so all kids had to do was play the game. They also went from almost fifteen hundred dollars to a hundred and fifty dollars. While that was still pretty expensive, it was a lot more affordable than the Atari. The most popular and innovative of these new consoles? The Nintendo Entertainment System, or NES for short. It was the console that every kid wanted, and most kids were able to get for Christmas or their birthday. With the debut of the game Super Mario Brothers steppong away from the normal games of Pong and Galactia, this thrilling console had kids of all ages, and even adults gathered around it to enjoy it. This further engulfed them into their anti-social bubbles as they were too engrossed in the games to go outside.

Video Games are blamed by many as being the downfall of modern society. That can be kind of seen as accurate, as there were so many people beginning to stay indoors rather than going outside. However, there were plenty of friendly people left in the world, and people still visited one another, so is this really the truth? Maybe as they progressed, but it was not an immediate destruction.

Media: This one can be brutal. People are so easily influenced by the media, that they could tell the people that Donald Trump farted unicorns, and they would almost believe it. Okay, maybe not that bad, but that is the general idea with the media. Nowadays, the media is filled with bombings, kidnappings and other fear mongering materials that it makes it hard to trust the people around you.

In the beginning, the news just stated that. The news. It gave news of the war if there was one, and news With all the fear inducing news, it makes it hard to want to even talk to anyone, because it seems as if everyone is a murderer now. This is not a conducive environment from the friendly ways of the past.

Media could be considered the downfall of the friendly atmosphere, as it seeds fear of the human race in your mind, and that is what seems to have closed people off from their natural chatty instincts.

Internet: The dawn of the internet saw a rise in introverts massively. It is no secret that the internet has taken over the minds of most of our youth. This goes hand in hand with the media, as it is the main source of all media output.

So those are some of the possible causes of why it is harder now to talk to people than it used to be. Of course, for some people it is harder than others. People with anxiety, or shyness have a hard time even talking to people that are deemed safe by people they trust. It isn't really caused by fear, just a nervousness that causes these people to clam up. Chances are, since you are reading this, you are one of these people.

Do not fret. This book will help you get through this.

However, be prepared. Sometimes it takes more than self help, and if your problem has deeper seated issues, you may want to get the help of a psychiatrist. If these tips do not help, it is best to seek the help of one if you wish to be more of a conversationalist, and it is essential for your mental and emotional health. There will be more on that at the end of this book.

Chapter 2

Secret Tips 1-2

Step One-Talking to Yourself

This may seem a little silly, but it really does help. Actually it is the easiest way to get over your shyness, as it is more awkward to talk to yourself than it is to talk to other people. You just have to get past the first hump of not wanting to look like a fool, and own it.

Go into a room with a mirror, start by offering your hand to shake and mime shaking hands with the person staring back at you while introducing yourself. This may feel a little weird, as there is not going to be a meeting of hands, due to you only having the conversation with yourself.

Once you get past the standard greeting it is time to hold a conversation. You can either say your mirrored self's responses or you can keep them in your head. This is where it can get tricky. You cannot think of specific to you answers, rather, you have to think of general answers, as you are not really the person you are talking to. Talk away as if there was an actual person holding a conversation with you. You can think of this as a live diary, but more civilized and social, as you don't want to spill your secrets to someone who is essentially standing in as a stranger.

Here is a little scenario to help you visualize what it would be like.

SCENARIO

Kelly had just finished reading *How to Talk to Anyone: Ten Secrets You Wish You Knew*, and she wanted to try out the first tip, which was called "Talking to Yourself". She stepped into her bathroom, and closed the door.

"Okay Kelly. You can do this. You have to become better at holding conversation, as your husband's job requires you to attend various social events with him."

Looking into the mirror she offered her hand to the cold glass, feeling slightly foolish.

"Hello, my name is Kelly. And you are?"

In her head, she planned the response.

I am Richard Simms. Pleasure to meet you, Kelly. She used her husband's boss's name as that was the one she was sure she knew.

"Pleasure to meet you too, sir. How are you and your wife and kids?"

They are doing well, as am I. How about your children?

"Oh no children yet sir. Wanting to get ahead financially first."

A great plan, I must say. Children are very expensive little buggers.

Kelly was interrupted then, as her husband walked into the bathroom.

"Who on Earth are you talking to?"

"I am practicing holding a conversation. I don't want to embarrass you tomorrow at the banquet." Kelly blushed.

"Awe, sweetheart, you could never embarrass me, but I appreciate the effort, and I am glad you are taking the steps necessary to better yourself. I am proud of you." Her husband kissed her forehead and left.

After that boost of confidence, Kelly found it much easier to practice her conversation skills, and felt less awkward about talking to herself in the mirror.

It may seem a little awkward to talk to yourself in a mirror, but after awhile it will be much easier, as you will start to feel better about helping yourself become the best that you can be. If someone comes in and asks you what you are doing, explain to them what you are trying to do. You never know, maybe they will try it for themselves.

Of course there is still a stigma that talking to yourself means that you are crazy, but once you explain that you are not trying to be weird, you just are trying to become better at conversation, people will understand. It is getting harder and harder for people to hold a normal conversation in this world, so it is always refreshing to hear that someone is trying to better themselves.

Step Two- Have a Few Ice Breakers

It is no secret that after the initial introductions conversation gets really awkward if there are no real conversation starters in the room. You say hello, state your name, and ask a few questions about what the person does, and how their day has been, but after that is over, this is when conversation dies out with a bunch of "Ums" and "Uhhh". Having a few ice breakers is always important as you can keep the conversation going, and often have a few laughs going at the end.

Of course it is hard to tell exactly what you should use as an ice breaker, and that is why most people have a hard time keeping the conversation going. However there are few fool proof ice breakers that will make talking to someone a breeze. This section will go over some ice breakers to use... and some to avoid.

Good Ice Breakers

Latest viral cat video: Pretty much everyone in the world loves cat videos, and a lot of people have seen them. Bringing that up in conversation is always a great way to push conversation along. It is a safe topic that won't offend people, and if someone hasn't seen the video, you can show it to them, eliciting a few laughs and smiles. Almost everyone loves cat videos.

Food: Everyone eats. So ask the person what kind of food they like. It is always pertinent to ask them first, because if they are vegan, you don't want to say "Bacon is the greatest, is it not?" Discuss different cuisines, and if they have not tried one of your favorites, suggest a good place to find it. Talking about food can bring people closer together, as they find common likes and interests in cuisines.

Music: Everyone listens to music. No matter what their tastes, everyone loves music. You cannot deny the fact that life would be boring without it. It fills the awkward silences, and it can bring up someone who is down. There is no escaping the fact that music is tied to emotions as well. Try asking the person what their favorite song is. Ask them the genres they like. If you find you have some interests that are similar, that is great, and that will further boost the conversation.

Hobbies: Everyone has a passion that probably has nothing to do with their job. Hobbies are what make life interesting. It is a safe topic to approach, because many people love to talk about what they enjoy, but rarely anyone asks.

Anything to do with interests: Pretty much anything to do with personal interests is safe to talk about, because people love to talk about themselves. They love to make known what they enjoy, and they love when someone shows interest in them. However, most people are too shy to actually talk about themselves unprompted because they do not wish to seem conceited.

Bad Ice Breakers

Politics: There are so many different opinions out there, and unfortunately with politics, everyone thinks that they are right. The conversation can get really awkward if you are a Democrat butting heads with a Republican. That is only the tip of the iceberg though. Tempers often flare at the slightest mention that either party may be corrupt, so it is best all around to just avoid the conversation entirely.

Religion: This is another one that is best avoided. Religion is a very sensitive subject for some, and no one wants someone else's religion shoved in their faces. That is why you are better off keeping this one put away.

Life choices: It is great that you have decided to become a vegan and all, but you do not have to convert everyone who is around you. Same with any of the life choices you make, whether you sell avon or those scammy weight loss products, pretty much no one wants to hear the spiel. Save it for if you are asked.

So there you have it. Some good, and bad, icebreakers to help you extend any conversation past the initial hello. Once you are able to establish a gateway to conversation, you will be able to carry on a lot easier than you would if you had not used an ice breaker at all, and were floundering about like a fish out of water, trying to figure out what to say.

How These Tips Help

These tips help you relax a little bit. They give you a little confidence boost, knowing that you are prepared to hold a conversation with people you may meet, because you have practiced the basics. It is a lot easier to do something once you have practiced it a few times.

It also helps you get past the awkwardness, as nothing is more awkward than holding a conversation with yourself. You will be able to talk to someone without feeling silly, because you couldn't possibly feel any more goofy than you did talking to a mirror.

Follow these tips to get the ball rolling on talking to people.

Chapter 3

Secret Tips 3-4

Now that you have gotten past the tips on how to approach and talk to someone, it is time to move on to the tips on how to hold a conversation. This is important, because starting a conversation is only a small part of the battle. This means that you have to be able to continue a conversation past the point of the ice breaker.

Conversations do not have to be hours long but you do have to keep them at a length that does not make you seem rude, or disinterested. If you only talk to someone about one subject and then leave, the person will feel as if they did something to offend you or something like that. You do not want to leave anyone feeling that way.

The best way to avoid that is to make sure that you keep the conversation going to the point where it would be safe to exit without offending the person you are talking too. This section will help you more understand how to keep a conversation going, and keep it going well.

Tip Three- Self Disclosure

To truly understand this tip, there is going to have to be some in depth explanation of what self disclosure is. To save you from having to look it up, this tip will include all the information you need to know about it. Of course that will make this tip a lot longer, but it is better to have a long tip that you understand, than a short briefing on something that leaves you confused.

Self disclosure is where you add to a conversation by giving the other person information about yourself. This is a hard thing to do, as most people worry about boring others with talk of themselves, or they are afraid to seem conceited.

There are two dimensions to self disclosure. They are breadth and depth. These are both essential to holding a good conversation, and connecting with the person you are talking to. You want to be able to connect with the people around you or else you will not be able to hold a true and meaningful conversation. You have to have both to truly enable the act of self disclosure.

Breadth of self disclosure refers to the range of topics you discuss when opening up about yourself. No you don't have to disclose your deepest darkest secrets, but giving someone a little bit of information about several different subjects about yourself allows them to feel a little closer to you, thus allowing them to open up about themselves. This helps extend the conversation and lets the person feel values, as if you really are interested in talking with them. Try starting with the easiest topics, such as interests, and move on to schooling, and views on the world. The more subjects you cover, the longer the conversation will be, and the more you will be able to connect with the person you are talking too.

Depth is slightly more difficult to reach. Now if you are just chatting up with someone you don't plan to develop a deep friendship with, you can almost skip depth, but a deep conversation is needed for those you wish to establish a true friendship with. However, even in a simple conversation, you need to have some depth to what you are saying. Tell them about the time you broke your arm in third grade, or something of the like. Give them a memory to really make them feel as if you care about the conversation you are having, and are not just shooting the breeze to pass time.

The act of self disclosure is a type of social penetration. This is a theory that you can only establish any type of relationship, whether it be romantic or platonic, by communication. But not just any type of communication, systematically fluid conversation. This means that over time, you let the person in more and more, and you change the direction of your conversation regularly to establish a connection with the person you are communicating with.

You also have to allow time for the person to reciprocate in the conversation. Don't spend the entire time talking about yourself. If you are worried about droning on too long about what you like and such, try employing the one detail method. This means that you share a detail about yourself, and let the other person share a detail about themselves. Continue this on until you find a happy medium between not sharing enough and talking too much.

As you can see self disclosure is very important, as you need to really allow a person to feel as if you are invested in the conversation. If you do not seem like you really care to talk to them, they will close off, and not want to talk much more than the basic hello followed by an ice breaker subject. So how do you efficiently employ this technique?

> Start Small: On top of them feeling like you are interested, they also have to be interested in what you have to say. Rather than unloading a whole pile of information on someone that doesn't really care, start with a small bit of information to see if they take the

bait. If you use the icebreaker about music, try telling them your favorite song, and explaining a basic reason for why you love it. If they just give you a one word reply, it is best to duck out of the conversation then. They don't really care. However, if they seem interested, and ask you more then you can start talking about more of your interests and such.

Decide on The Type of Conversation: You should always try to approach every conversation as if you are trying to make a new friend. However, if you are at a convention with people from around the globe, chances are you are not going to establish a life long friendship. You should still show interest in the person, but that would definitely impact the type of information that you are going to divulge. You don't want someone you are never going to see again knowing a deep secret about you. Instead tell them about childhood memories that you don't feel would impact how they think of you. Your favorite thing to do as a child or things like that. Those are safe subjects for people who you are just talking to in that moment.

Skim the Surface: You want people to be interested in you for a long time. This means that you cannot divulge everything about you in one conversation. You have to be conservative with your information. The best way to do this is to take a little bit of information from many different subjects to talk about. As you get to know a person more and more, you can add more information to that. This helps you also ensure that you are not talking about yourself too much.

Allow Reciprocation: The best part of self disclosure is that it allows the other person a gateway to talk about themselves as well. You don't want to hog the stage and only talk about yourself. You want to keep the flow of information even. Give the other person some time to tell you about themselves as well. Conversation will come alight as you are swapping stories and some fun little tidbits of information about yourself.

Be Loose: Telling someone about yourself should be done with ease. You don't want to sound like someone who is selling something, though in reality that is what you are doing in a way. You are trying to convince the person to like you with the truth. However, it should not sound like you are a documentary. You should be light and airy when talking about yourself. Make the person interested. Intrigue them, and draw them in, make them want to know more about you.

Timing: Just like when you deliver the punchline to a joke, it is all about the timing. You have to time the information that you deliver. This is a little tricky if you don't know what goes into timing a deliverance. There has to be a level of interest from the other person. To ensure that you have their interest, you have to make them ask a few questions. You can't just offer up all the information. However, you can't make them pry every bit of info from you either. There has to be a give and take kind of flow going on there.

Caution: There are some things that you do not tell a person you just met. It may seem like you have known the person forever, but you still have to use caution when divulging certain things. For example, if you were a former addict, it is best to not mention it unless absolutely necessary. You do not want anything to skew how they think of you until they get to know you. If you are confident in yourself however, then try divulging that info. What you are cautious with depends on you.

There you have it. Self disclosure at its finest. This is one of the most important things to holding a good conversation. Now remember, your entire conversation does not have to consist of self disclosure alone, but throwing in a few facts here and there go a long way. Make sure you utilize this to the fullest advantage possible.

Tip Four- Engage the Other Person Fully

Part of the problem these days is that conversation becomes one sided. Even though both parties are speaking, they are not really in the conversation. They are not properly engaging the other person. This is a big issue, when conversation relies entirely on both parties being actively engaged in the conversation to allow it to succeed. If you are not actively engaging the other person, and not engaged yourself, then you will fall flat in the conversation.

First off, how you can be engaged in the conversation better, without taking it over.

> Actively Listen: No one wants to feel like they are talking to a brick wall. They want to feel like the person they are talking to is genuinely interested in what they have to say. This means that you have to listen to understand. Today's generation teaches you to listen to reply, and that is where the problem lies. By only listening to reply, you are not processing what they person is saying, because your mind is on yourself. This is a selfish, bad habit that this day and age has taken to sticking too.

> Reply with Interest: Even if you are not quite interested in what the other person is talking about,

you should always reply with interest. It is polite, and even though you may not be interested in it now, you might gain some interesting knowledge by listening to what they have to say. You can't just expect everyone to have the same interests as you, and there are probably things that you like that others do not like but they still act like they are at least interested in it, because it is the polite thing to do.

Ask Questions: Asking questions to get more information about what they are talking about shows the other person that you were listening, and that you want to know more. It allows the person to be relieved, because then they do not feel like they are boring you with their information. The only way that they know that you are interested is if you are asking questions. Then they know that it is okay to continue talking about the subject they are on.

Be THERE: I know it can be hard if someone is droning on and on about something that you have no interest in, but it is still good etiquette to be there mentally. This means that when someone is talking, don't let your mind go on vacation, and tune the person out, because if you are that disinterested in them it is more polite to change the subject rather than just leave the conversation mentally.

That is how you can be engaged in a conversation. Following these tips will allow you to breathe easier knowing that you are pleasantly talking to a person, and you wont offend them because you seem disinterested. You just have to practice these things, because sometimes it can be a little difficult.

How to Engage Them

Be Interesting: This does not mean you have to make up stories. It has nothing to do with the information you are giving at all. You just have to deliver it in an interesting way. You could tell someone you climbed mount Everest on the back of Dwayne Johnson, and if you tell the story in a monotone voice, it will sound boring. It is not what you are saying, it is how you are saying. Tell them your stories as if you were telling them for the first time. Be engaged yourself, and show the person that you want them to talk to you. You want their attention. Only then will you get the attention you so desire.

Leave Openings: Even without using self disclosure, you still have to leave openings for the other person to talk, no matter the subject. No one wants to stand there and listen to someone take control of the conversation. You might as well be talking to yourself for that matter. Or to the plant in the corner. You have to let the other person talk as well. A good conversation allows both parties to talk equally, and without any hitches. It is not one person talking about everything while the other person stands there and nods.

Allow Questions: If a person asks a question, don't dodge it. This should not have to be said, but a lot of people dodge questions for fear of sounding conceited, but in truth you just seem rude. If someone is asking a question, you are not going to sound conceited by answering it. If you dodge a question, the person will feel as if they offended you, and they will be less likely to stay engaged in the conversation.

That is how you engage someone in conversation. It is a lot easier than staying engaged in a conversation as long as they are interested in what is being said. All you have to do is be open and friendly, and let the rest fall into place.

How These Tips Help

These tips are designed to help you keep a conversation going without being nervous. These tips also help improve your communication skills. By using these tips you will feel more comfortable having a longer conversation with someone that you just met, than you would be if you were just trying to find things to talk about.

These tips will give you the boost you need to feel confident in your abilities to talk to people and really enjoy the conversation without having to worry every second that you are saying something wrong.

Chapter 4

Secret Tips 5-6

These tips are for what you should do during and after a conversation with someone. They are tips on how to properly act when communicating, as there is often some confusion on what to do. Especially now that it is no longer a curriculum at school or home. Do not fret. This book will clarify that right up.

Tip Five- Etiquette During a Convo

It is of utmost importance that you have the proper etiquette when talking to someone. The key to holding a good conversation is to not offend them, and to show them that you are a good person to talk to. You want to hold their attention and let them know that they have yours. Otherwise you will not get very far in the communication realm, as people will not want to talk to you, thinking you are rude.

So it is best to study up on proper etiquette before you put yourself out there. While most of these are common sense, they are in here just in case nerves cause a problem with combining common sense with communication. That is a real problem a lot of people have. They cannot rely on their common sense because they are too nervous to remember to use it.

So here are the etiquette rules to help you out. Remember, a slip up is okay as long as you don't do it continually, but it is best to try to be as clean cut as possible to avoid any issues.

    Handshake: This is the first thing you should do, as you say hello. Unless the person is germaphobic, or you are, not offering a handshake is considered rude. If you do have a phobia of germs, it is best to explain that as you are saying hello, so there are no misunderstandings. Make sure that they know that you are still pleased to meet them, you just would rather not shake their hand. Most people can be pretty understanding.

The perfect handshake is firm, but pliant. You can't grip too tight, because you are not trying to intimidate someone, and a grip too loose makes people feel that you are not that thrilled to meet them, and are only doing so out of necessity. This is not a great first impression, as people want to feel like they are worth getting to know. So it is best to make sure you give a good, true handshake.

Eye Contact: This one is important to maintain from the beginning to end. It is always disconcerting to talk to someone who is looking off in the distance or anywhere else but who is talking to them. (autistic people are not counted in this, nor are the ocularly impaired) Eye contact shows that you are paying attention to them. To show you why eye contact is so important, let us have a mini history lesson.

Back in the time of extreme social hierarchy, where people who made less money than you were deemed undesirable, eye contact was a way of establishing that social ladder. Anyone who was deemed below you had to make eye contact with you, while you were not to make eye contact with them. To make eye contact with a person deemed lowly, put you on their level, and could cause you to lose your social position if caught.

Kings never looked anyone but other kings in the eye, no one ever made eye contact with serfs other than other serfs. Men did not make eye contact with women, as even women were deemed below them. They only time someone made eye contact with a woman that was not another woman, was a servant, or a peasant to a duchess or queen. Eye contact was the main factor of social hierachy

By not looking someone in the eye during conversation, you are essentially saying that they are beneath you, and that what they have to say is not important. That may not be what you are trying to do, but that is the message you are portraying when you refuse to look someone in the eye.

Body Language: This will be more brushed on in a later chapter, but it also falls under etiquette. You have to have an open body language in a conversation, otherwise you risk making a person feel as if you are unapproachable, and not open to conversation. You can also make them feel as if what they are saying has no value. You can do so much damage with a few simple gestures, and this is a problem. You have to be careful with your stance and make sure that you are not closing yourself off.

No Phone: This should go without saying, but if your phone goes off, DON'T ANSWER IT! Society today is so caught up in the conversations that they have going on on the other side of the screen, that they forget the importance of conversation with the person on the other side of the table. You are in a real time conversation with a real person. (Not that the person texting you isn't real, but they are not there.) The best thing to do is to put your phone on silent if you know you are going to talk to people. That way you do not feel tempted to pull it out and text rather than talking to those around you.

Cell phones are a wonderfully destructive device. They can help you connect with people from around the world, but unfortunately that causes you to disconnect from the people that are right next to you. A lot of people use their phone as a crutch to not have to talk to people when they feel uncomfortable. This does not help you in any way. They only way to become comfortable with a situation is to put yourself out there, and talk to people. Find someone to talk to and eventually you will take your mind off of the fact that you are anxious about being around people.

Don't Interrupt: When someone is talking to you, it is best to stay quiet until you are sure they have finished what they are saying. You have to be very careful when talking to someone that you are listening to them, and not listening to respond. This is one of the biggest problem in today's conversations. No one listens to people for more than knowing when to jump in and reply. This leads to more people interrupting, which often angers the other person, and makes them not want to talk to you any longer.

Listen to the person, and remember that you would not want to be interrupted. No one likes to be talked over, and no one likes talking to someone who constantly does it. Be patient. Your time to talk will come.

> Personal Space: This is a big one. A lot of people get really close to people when they are talking. This is uncomfortable for the other person. You have to make sure that you keep a good distance between you and the

other person. Arm's length apart is generally a good chatting distance unless you are in a loud place, and then from forearm length apart is generally as close as you should be. If it is too loud to hear then, maybe hold the conversation until you are in a quieter environment.

Claustrophobia is a big problem for a large majority of a population. Invading someone's personal space can make them very uncomfortable. You have to respect that people need personal space when talking to you. Even if they don't have claustrophobia, it is still gross when someone is so close to you that you can feel their spit as they are talking. Keep the distance.

> Get Close: This may seem contradicting to the last statement, but you have to be close enough that it does not look like you are trying to escape the conversation. However, it is not that contradictory. You just have to find a happy medium. You want to be close enough that the other person is not sniffing themselves trying to

figure out if it is them, but you have to be far enough away that you are not crowding their personal space.

A good indicator is your arms. Of course you do not physically stretch them out to see if you are standing close enough, but rather you visualize where you are at. You should never so close that you have to bend your arm at more than a ninety degree angle to touch them, but you should not be so far away that when your arms are fully outstretched your palms can't rest on their shoulders. Try to stay in that golden circle of space, and you should be good.

Those are the tips for etiquette during a conversation. Follow these, and you should have no problem with people not wanting to talk to you. You will make the other person feel respected, and that is what you are striving for.

Tip Six- Etiquette When Leaving a Conversation

Timing: As stated before, timing is everything when talking to people. You have to be good at your timing and actually know when to say something when not to say something. In this case, timing has to do with when to exit a conversation. No matter how good a conversation has been, you begin to wear out your welcome. If a person starts to look around or shift about, they are probably ready to go, or do something else. This is your cue to end the conversation if they do not. Finish what you were saying, and then use an exit phrase such as "Oh I can't believe how much of your time I have taken! It was so great talking to you I just got swept up in the moment!" Make them feel good while ending the conversation.

> Ending Phrase: As mentioned in the above bullet, you have to use a good ending phrase to make the person feel as if the conversation ending is not their fault, even if it is. Be polite, and make them feel like you were so enthralled by talking to them that you regret having to end the conversation, but you do not want to take up

any more of their time. This will make them feel valued, and that will make them want to talk to you again.

Ask for Contact Info: If you have the chance of seeing someone again, or just would like to stay in touch, ask if they would like to exchange contact information. If they say yes, go ahead and give them your number and ask for theirs, giving a test call to make sure you input the number right, and allowing them to be sure of the same, as the will have your number from the call. If they do not wish to exchange information, do not push. It doesn't mean you did anything wrong, they just may not think that they will see you again. That is okay.

Always ask if they want to exchange information. It is a lot more comfortable for them, as it gives them a little more room to say no without feeling bad. Asking them for their contact information directly does not allow for them to say no without feeling bad, because you assumed that they wanted to. Remember, good conversation does not mean they have to become your best friend. A lot of people become so attached to someone they had a single enthralling conversation with, that they are upset when the person does not want to keep in touch. This is simple human nature, as we are designed to communicate for survival. Breaking yourself of this habit will be difficult, but if you do it, you will be less affected by the rejection you feel when someone does not wish to stay in touch.

Follow Up: This only refers to people who exchanged info. If they give you their contact information, then text or call them the next day to see how they are doing and let them know that you were serious about wanting to stay in touch. Make the person feel important, but only text once, and let them respond. They might be busy when you try to reach them, and will get back to you later.

These are the etiquette rules for ending a conversation. If you use them, you can be confident that you are not leaving someone with awkwardness in the air.

How These Tips Help

These tips give you the boost up in a conversation to show a person that you are respectful, and that you have proper manners. This will make them enjoy talking to you a lot better than if you did not know these rules.

Etiquette is slowly slipping away, by trying to bring it back, you will also start a ripple effect, as the person you are talking to will pick up on these social cues, and start using them in their conversations with others. By doing this little simple thing, you can help bring proper conversation etiquette back into a trend.

Chapter 5

Secret Tips 7-10

These tips are just extra tips that you should know and insert throughout different conversations. They do not necessarily have to apply to every conversation, as they are not about the conversation itself, but how to psych yourself up to talk to people, and how to handle rejection without letting it ruin you.

Tip Seven- Get Out of Your Head

You have to get out of your own head to ever hold a good conversation with someone, because you have to be able to approach someone to talk to them. If you are stuck in your head, and the "Oh I can't" thoughts, then you will be stuck at only talking to people you have to.

By getting out of your head, you will feel confident enough to approach a person that you have never met before, and that has no correlation to any of your friends. This is the best feeling, knowing that you can make friends anywhere, and not have to worry about going somewhere and not knowing anyone there.

Imagine you are going to a party. Your friend says that they will meet you there. You are glad, because you don't know anyone else who will be attending, or they are just minor acquaintances from work or school. You get there, and your friend texts you saying that they can't come because something came up. You don't panic because you decide to just go find someone to talk to. You walk up to a guy or girl you have never seen before, and strike up a conversation.

Before the night is up, you have met seven new people that you really get along with.

That is what can happen once you stop the thoughts that you aren't good enough to talk to someone, or that you are too boring for anyone to want to talk to. Confidence is key. Boost yourself up, and as they say, fake it till you make it. You have to boost yourself up, because there is not going to be anyone in the world who is able to make you feel better about yourself than you can. Go in with the mindset that you are worth talking to, and that you are funny, and witty. By believing in yourself, people will be more open to you, as they can see that you are confident in yourself.

Tip Eight- Boost Your Self Esteem

This one goes hand in hand with getting out of your head. You have to believe in yourself to get out of your head. If you have low self esteem, you will be more prone to rejection, because just like lions, people can pick out the meek ones. No one wants to have to carry the entire conversation, so they generally steer away from the shy people, and gravitate to someone who they know will actively engage in conversation.

The way to boost your self esteem can also involve a mirror. Stand in front of it for ten minutes a day only saying positive things about yourself. You are smart, you are strong, you are caring, you are kind. Do not mention any of your negative attributes. For every negative thing you say, add another minute to the time you spend looking in the mirror. It is your responsibility to build yourself up, no one else's. You can do it. As the days go on, you will find you are having to add less time onto your ten minutes, until finally, you spend just the ten minutes saying completely positive things about yourself. Eventually you will begin to believe them. You are essentially retraining your brain to say nice things to you, rather than mean things.

This society is so bleak, and there are so many mean people who say hateful things while hiding behind a computer screen, and this has cause self esteem rates to go way down. Build yourself back up to stay above the hatred

Tip Nine- Handle Rejection with Pride

If you have low self esteem, this will be hard, so you have to build yourself up to be able to do this. Otherwise, it will get to you , and make you not want to talk to people any longer. If you are rejected before you build yourself up, just take some time to recuperate.

Not everyone will want to talk to you, especially nowadays. In today's age, people judge others before they even open their mouths, and decide on if a person is "worthy" of speaking to them. You have to break away from this thinking. You also cannot think that someone is above your level, they may seem like they are, and turn out to be the nicest person ever. However, when you approach someone, they may reject you, and this is okay. You may not want to talk to every person that approaches you either.

If you are rejected, shake it off. Remind yourself that it is not you, it is who they are. They decided that they did not want to get to know you, and that is their loss, not yours. Get back up on that metaphorical horse and try again with someone else. You will find someone who is actually worth talking to.

Tip Ten- Don't Latch On

In a setting with a lot of people, it is so easy to try to find one person that you enjoy talking to, and staying with them a majority of the time. This is a bad idea. You have to work the crowd so to speak. How boring would it be if you were at a concert, and the singer only interacted with one fan. It is the same concept with talking to people. Go around to different people, and try to make more than one new friend. Eventually you can come back to that one person, but let them have some time to talk to others, and give yourself time to talk to others as well.

How These Tips Help

These tips are for your own personal use to adapt to specific conversations and situation, and to psych yourself up before you go to a social event where you may not know someone that is there.

Following these tips will give you an edge on your

conversations. Using these will help give you a self esteem boost, and you will learn how to help yourself. These tips will make you a better conversationalist and a better you.

Chapter 6

Bonus Tips

If you have tried all of these tips, and find that you still cannot connect with people, you should try to see about getting some help with a psychiatrist. There could be some real deep-seated issues there. Talking to people is hard, but if you have tried to break out of your shell, and find yourself having panic attacks every time, you need to find out what is going wrong.

There is nothing wrong with getting help either. Just as you would need to see a doctor for a physical illness, you should see a psychiatrist if your social anxiety is so bad that it is causing you to break down at the thought of talking to someone you do not know. There are a lot of resources that are at your disposal. If you do not know a psychiatrist in your area, try talking to your normal doctor, and he can help refer you to someone. The best thing about that, is he is more likely to know a specialist to ensure that you are getting the best level of help that you can get.

How to know if it is more than just being shy

> You have panic attacks regularly in social situations: This can be the sign of a serious problem. You should get it checked out, and maybe the doctor can help you figure out how to work through it in a way that is best suited to you.
>
> You avoid stores during busy hours: If you would rather go without a necessity for a period of time because you do not want to visit a store during busy hours as there will be too many people there, and could cause you to have a meltdown, you should see a doctor. This is serious. You cannot deny your needs. A doctor can help you figure out the root of the problem, and set you on your way to healing.

If you feel physically ill in social situations where there are only a handful of people: If being in small groups makes you feel physically ill, you should definitely look into it. Doing so allows you to truly live your life to the fullest, once you figure out what is wrong.

Don't let anxiety control your life any longer. Get the help you deserve, and do not feel bad for doing so. You deserve to live a happy life unrestrained by anxiety. Regain control of your life.

INTRODUCTION
REIGNITE YOUR RELATIONSHIP

Carol and Alex have been together for seven years now, and yet it feels like twenty. Their son is in kindergarten, and the baby is just at the age where she's getting into everything. Outside of his full-time job as a contractor, Alex acts as a handyman on the side in hopes of saving the down payment for a new home. Carol telecommutes from home so she can be there for the kids and avoid the high cost of daycare. Although Carol and Alex are emotionally bonded, their sex life leaves much to be desired—literally. What started out as "hot and heavy," is now a weekend quickie between HBO and streaming Facebook.

Even though Alex and Carol agree their sexual relationship needs a reboot, they have no idea how to recapture their initial fire. They have managed to have sex a few times a month, but more times than not, it's more duty than dazzling. At first, they tried to reassure one another by promising sex tomorrow, when they'd had more sleep or when the kids went to grandmas. The problem was, tomorrow never came.

What Carol and Alex need are some help building a fire beneath their waning sexual relationship. At this point, it's going to take more than a match stroke over kindling to reeve up their sexual appetites. This one's going to need a "five-star" fire up—or should I say a "Five Key" fire up? Can you relate? Before you've finished reading about the "Five Keys," you and your partner will be sitting down this book and giving each one of them a try.

Between these pages, we will present proven strategies and practices designed to get you back on track to an incredible sexual relationship. After reading this book, you'll be wanting more—sex, that is. These Five Keys will give you so much fire in your sex life that you'll soon burn through all those bad habits you've created and release your inner sexual beast.

Oh, that got your attention, didn't it? If you found yourself shaking your head in agreement when hearing of the decrease in sexual appetite between Carol and Alex, you'll be encouraged to know that most all decreases or dysfunctions are fixable. Your sexual issues might be caused by completely different things, but the pain and hurt suffered from the lack of good sex are the same. These "Five Keys" will not only examine what could be causing your problems but will also give you practical "how to" steps to take you and your partner to a whole new sexual high. By believing in and embracing the Five Keys to light up your sexual experiences, you can expect…

- More intimacy in your relationship

- Better communication of your needs and wants

- Greater physical prowess

- Closer emotional connection

- More confidence and self-esteem

- Fewer suspicions and doubts regarding your partner

- More energy and sexual desire

- Better overall health and well-being

- Flat out—more hot sex

These five powerful Keys to reigniting your sexual fires will teach you how to reset your sexual expectations. You'll begin to see yourself as a dynamic lover and nurturing partner. As we break down each Key element to reigniting your sexual fires, you'll discover more creative and mysterious ways to please your partner and yourself. They'll teach you how to build anticipation for your next sexual encounter. Who knows, you and your lover will probably adopt this as your next "in bed" read.

Communication is everything, including how you speak with your body as well as your words. Powerful physical messages can be sent without ever saying a word. Like a moth to a flame, your partner will soon want to see what this new you is all about. As you learn more about yourself, you'll be able to more effectively communicate to your partner what to do to make you tremble with anticipation.

Notice, so far, we've talked about "building" the fire. Like every fire, it begins with a spark of promise, interest, and curiosity. To build a true fire, that spark must be tended to, fanned, and heaped with materials to create a rising flame. If you fail to tend to the fire constantly, it goes out. If you cover the fire with the sands of judgment, stress, doubt, and fear, your fire will be distinguished before it's had a chance to heat up your sex life.

Before you know it, instead of giving a stranger that sexually charged look or experience that fiery glow from an eye-to-eye light from a passer-by, you'll be eagerly waiting in the bedroom for your lover to come to bed—if you make it to the bedroom. The Keys will provide playful and exciting ways to motivate yourself and your partner to engage in more creative sex. I'm not talking about the legs-over-your-head kind of sex unless of course, that's your turn-on. I'm talking about ways that engage your mind as well as your body. The Keys show you how to be fully committed—how to give sex the full-Monty treatment.

From learning to please yourself to giving the "let's have hot sex" signal to your partner, discovering the importance of timing and mounting anticipation is crucial. There are perfect times to have sex, and then there are perfect times to have naughty sex. There are proper places to have sex, and then there are under-the-table places to share hidden sexual activities. Having fun and being creative is not an option; it's a necessity.

So, are you "up" for this? You will be, especially when you learn these Five Keys and apply them to your sex life.

PART II

Spoken communication, even in the digital age, still stands as the most important way in which we interact with one another. Conversations trump other forms of communications such as texts and emails because unlike these less personal, digital forms, they offer the chance to make in-game adjustments in the present moment. When we exchange ideas and express our concerns in conversation it can be something of a chess match. We want our 'moves' to ultimately create successful outcomes with the result of the conversation giving us what we hoped to accomplish. Before the conversation begins, we must give consideration to some important criteria – who it is we're talking to, what it is we want out of the conversation, and how will we prepare ourselves to have the conversation. We have to give some thought to these before considering the tactics we will employ as it is impractical to take a 'kitchen sink' approach to every conversation. The most effective conversation tactics are centered around wit, composure, politeness, consideration, flexibility, and guidance. These collectively help us to maintain quiet control over the conversation and enhance the probability that it will reach a positive conclusion. Conversations should build on one another and one way to gauge the direction of momentum is to have a brief follow-up for assurance that things are headed in the right direction.

CHAPTER 1: WHO ARE YOU TALKING TO?

For our purposes, a conversation is an exchange of verbally communicated ideas between two people. One of them is you, and the other is someone else. What is the degree of familiarity? Is it someone you've known all your life or is it that new co-worker that has been in the office for only a week? The relationship between those in the conversation helps establish a logical starting point.

An exchange between people who have only known each other professionally usually begins more formally than talk between two people who only know each other outside of their professional lives. It's appropriate to have 'small talk' precede the main focus in professional conversations due to the fact that people don't interact as often when this is the nature of the relationship and there are more uncertainties about one another.

With respect to personal relationships, there is a difference between what we shall call simple relationships and invested relationships.

Because relationships have the potential to evolve, connections might be transitioning from simple to a more complex relationship such as that of a someone we've started to date or perhaps a new mother-in-law. In instances of changing connections, the capital and the stakes of conversations usually increase in value.

Certainly there are instances where two people are connected both personally and professionally, sometimes for a long period of time. Playing golf with business partners is a scenario that could lead to such a situation. This can be a little complicated, and one or both may tend to suspend the rules of engagement due to familiarity. This may require backing up and trying to have more formally constructed conversation.

If the person you're conversing with is someone new to you, it's really important to know yourself well and be aware of any personal tendencies or personality traits that might be perceived as 'a bit much' until others get to know you. Most of us can think of a personality quirk for just about anybody we know, including ourselves. Others who know us well have likely offered constructive criticism of the more challenging aspects of our personality and we should take this to heart.

CHAPTER 2: WHAT ARE YOUR MOTIVATIONS?

Any conversation has a purpose. Perhaps it is simply to maintain good relations in an established friendship. We engage in many conversations with no real purpose or objective in mind other than to maintain connection a light-hearted connection – as in the one we have perhaps with someone who we encounter once a week or so that works the check-out line in the grocery store.

Conversations don't always have a destination to be reached or some other tangible outcome, depending upon the nature of the relationship. Simple relationships such as with someone working the check-out line with who we might have a brief conversation in passing are quite different from more invested relationships, such as that with a romantic companion, relative, or professional colleague. Our motivations for engagement vary here and we need to have at least a small appreciation for the purpose, lest we lose track of what we might have invested.

Romantic and business conversations, different as they may be in terms of topics, tone, and other attributes of communication do have in common that we are talking about some level of investment on our part and presumably on the part of someone else as well. Whether it's someone we're thinking about proposing marriage or a merger, there's a lot of investment in either case.

All invested conversations require that the wants, needs, and demands of one person be measured alongside those of the other. Are you asking someone to help your business grow by offering an innovative analysis of sales data? Are you persuading your spouse that it's time for the family to grow with the addition of another child? An inventory will need to be taken in either scenario of the points that are shared in addition to where there are differences. Unless something goes terribly wrong and invested relationships dissolve, conversations will continue to occur and should reflect an effort on the part of two people to recall and maintain an awareness of what they are asking of each other.

CHAPTER 3: HOW WILL YOU PREPARE?

When a meeting is scheduled or a date is on the calendar, there is often much anticipation about how things will go. Anticipation leads to expectation or in some cases, reservation. Going over the possible outcomes in your mind followed up by a rehearsal or mock conversation is a good way to cover your bases and provide a sense of confidence about the impending conversation. If someone else is not available, read a dialogue with several exchanges as means to warm up before the actual conversation takes place

A number of variables can come into play that would affect preparation. A lot depends on whether the conversation taking place is between people in a new versus existing relationship. If the other person is new to you, other than being resourceful and gleaning some pertinent facts for conversation fodder, about all you can do is have some topics in mind in the event that the conversation stalls.

If you have the benefit of having past conversations with someone, this is helpful in that you can recall how that person tends to engage with you. Will they lead the conversation if you give them the chance or will they defer? In the cases where there is familiarity, more preparation will have to be put into a conversation that is anticipated to be strained. For instance, if conflict resolution is a likely aspect, think of appropriate questions ahead of time and ways to address issues that diffuse tension, and create a more relaxed environment. Think about acknowledging differences up front using a reconciliatory tone.

CHAPTER 4: WHICH TACTICS ARE INDISPENSABLE?

So we're at the point where introductions and small talk are over. From start to end, there are multiple tactics than can be employed to enhance the outcome, much like playing a hand of cards in a timely fashion.

Starting a conversation in amicable fashion is critical. Cut the small talk short or eliminate it if the other person is short on time or simply prefers to get down to business in short order. If it is your first conversation with someone, be mindful that you never get a second chance to make a first impression, and that impression, be it fair or not, may be formed very quickly. Early on acknowledge the other party's interests or concerns prior to stating your own, if you are the one to open things up or lead the conversation.

From start to finish, be constantly mindful and feel things out on everything from the tone of the conversation to how the other person is reacting. If a conversation gets out of hand or veers off course very far, it may be difficult to achieve the original goals that were set out. Quietly ask yourself "is everything going well, or should I try to make an adjustment?" If the other person stumbles or seems confused about how things are proceeding, try to improve clarity so that both of you are confident about how things are going relative to what might have been anticipated.

Being perceived as focused and giving the other person your full attention is perhaps the most important characteristic of someone who has productive conversations. If you come across as aloof or distracted it will probably be a downer. Someone may have taken a significant chunk of time out of their day to set aside for what they thought was going to be a meaningful exchange and instead they are totally deflated by someone who seems somewhere else.

We have already shed light on coming up with appropriate questions in advance for what are anticipated to be challenging conversations. This is particularly true if modern electronic communication or social media exchanges have preceded or led to the conversation. Incomplete thoughts or confusion created by these shorthand approaches to communicating may result in questions that should be dealt with at the beginning of the conversation. Heck, they may be the entire reason for the conversation. Giving prior thought to appropriate questions is good in any case as the most relevant questions may not come to mind if you wait until the conversation has begun. It is likely that the most curious questions, which reflect serious thought on your part, will come up in advance. Modify questions if you perhaps initially asked something too broad.

Maintain composure rather than get defensive when someone is confrontational or insulting. Disarming someone with a witty or playful response give you the control that they forfeited by deploying counterproductive language.

Give thorough responses that indicate you have respect for other peoples' questions. Abbreviated or literal responses in addition to being insufficiently clear, may also suggest a lack of respect or consideration for what the other person is trying to learn. If their facial expression or other observable response suggests that they did not get the information they were wanting, politely ask them to clarify what they were asking for if it is not abundantly clear.

Be mindful of where the conversation is going and be ready to get it back on track if it is headed into unproductive or counterproductive turf. Be prepared to usurp the role of leading the conversation should it stall. The other person might not be inclined to take the initiative here, and you may have no way of knowing if they're new to you.

Just like you shouldn't give a literal or abbreviated response, you shouldn't ask questions that would lead someone to think you were asking for such. Questions that demand responses beyond the mundane will give the other person a chance to share a more detailed account leaving them feeling as though they got to share the whole story.

People want to be recognized and given due credit. Do yourself a favor and take the opportunity in advance. If they feel the need to bring attention to an accomplishment before you mention it, they are indicating that they feel a lack of respect. Recognition will make future conversations more productive because validation will motivate people to be more engaged.

We need to listen effectively in order to gain the respect of those we engage in conversation. Constantly cutting them off or interrupting them will make it seem as we are dismissing their importance in the relationship. One is not listening effectively if they are unable to stay in the present moment. Diverting the conversation may also be regarded as not respecting someone's concern about the topic at hand.

Making demands or requests in a conversation is a sensitive matter. Be fair and don't ask for too much. Don't ask for something if it is going to be obvious that you haven't done anything to help yourself and just want to place a burden on the other person. No one wants to feel as though they're being taken advantage of, so consider carefully as to whether you should make a request of them.

Demonstrate that you are in the moment by actions that are visibly obvious. Record notes during the conversation or commitments you have made. Place a future date on your phone calendar when an event is mentioned. This implies intent on your part to follow through and makes the other person feel as though they've gotten something across to you and that their input was worthwhile.

CHAPTER 5: THE SUPREME TACTIC – THE FOLLOW-UP

CONVERSATION

After a conversation, you must take inventory of how things went. If you know of strategic mistakes that were made along the way, make note of them and take care not to commit them in future conversations. You must hold yourself responsible for being able to recall any specific outcomes and good note-taking is the best way to accomplish this. If a conversation ends with both parties knowing what was specifically agreed to or are certain of specific commitments that were made and how outcomes are to be achieved, it may not be necessary to revisit the conversation down the road. When outcomes aren't certain and nothing was specifically agreed upon, it may be in the best interest of two people to come back together and express their views about what each took from the conversation. Revisit the points of agreement and disagreement with emphasis given as to why sentiments differed on particular subjects that were discussed. An apologetic tone might be called for if you lost your composure or you felt deficient in attention or focus. Remember that follow-up conversation may be used as a polite gesture to offer thanks or appreciation, in which case they needn't be extended affairs. If a follow-up is something of an in-between linking two major conversations, it may require more input as it establishes what will be discussed in the latter conversation.

PART III

Chapter 1

How Technology Has Affected Our Communication Skills

Before we dive into the practical strategies of overcoming those dreaded awkward moments, there is some basic information that you should know. You see, it is my belief that seeing a full picture of the context will help you to understand the basis of your communication block better.

In truth, the world we live in today is a lot different than it used to be back in the days of covered wagons and community bathing. Yuck! It is certainly better in a myriad of ways. We have the technology, fast cars, airplanes, hell even indoor plumbing! But. Just but. It isn't better in some respects.

We Were Set Up To Fail

You see, people call this the age of communication. People call this the golden era of instant connectivity based on the ease in which we can talk to people hundreds or even thousands of miles away from us. That is certainly a great thing in all but wait. What about the people that are sitting right next to us? How connected to them are we?

Over seventy percent of the world's population admits to having a problem with communicating properly with people in their families. Think about that for a moment. SEVENTY PERCENT! That is just mind boggling. And to put things into perspective, more than three out of four of your neighbors probably face this same issue as you do.

It is also faithful to a vast extent that a consequence of that problem leads to one not having the proper communication skills to engage on a personal level with strangers or primary acquaintances.

Have you noticed that in the past, before telephones were in every household, it was so much easier to talk to people face to face? That is because for the longest time, excluding the post that came every week or the occasional messenger pigeon that often took days to reach a destination seventy miles away, it was the **only** form of communication with someone! If you wanted to have a full conversation in real time with someone you knew that wasn't living in your own home you had to move your butt up from your seat, walk over to their house, knock on their door, open your mouth, and talk to them. Sounds harsh eh? Now think how many people do that now in the modern age.

This meant that communication was futile to survival in the past. If you needed something from someone, you had to physically and verbally ask for it. This also meant that you would have to communicate regularly with everyone around you to get stuff done.

Past Customs Allowed For Natural Conversations

In the past, it was customary to greet everyone with a smile when you're walking down the street. Not doing so was considered bad manners. In contrast, people living in the modern age are so glued to their smartphones or listening to their music with earphones shoved deep down their ear drums that their mouths don't even move much anymore. People are LESS connected to one another today.

In the past humans had to interact by speaking several times a day and as a result, people were not only more friendly to one another, they became more fluent and natural at talking and communicating with their peers. They had proper training on a daily basis just by opening their mouths more often. How easy is that?

We Were Not Given The Chance To Develop Our Social Skills

You see, children in days gone by were taught from a young age how to socialize. They were sent outside to make their friends, and they were taught how to be self-sufficient. This gave them the confidence to speak to others. In school, they were instructed on what appropriate conversation was. Children were often taught not to speak unless spoken to. This was to teach them to listen to those around them truly and to respond in a meaningful and understanding way. This training not only made them good listeners but also compassionate adults that were able to hold productive conversations in the highest of social settings. As you can see, a conversation was key to survival.

Where's The Social Gathering In The Modern Age?

Let's face it. We are all glued to our smartphones, tablets, and computers. Swiping left on Tinder, surfing the net, texting people on Facebook or iMessage. When have we ever had a decent conversation or a happy get-together with our closest friends? The truth is that we were crippled by our devices the day we got them. It is unfortunate now, isn't it?

Consequences Of Rapid Development

The hectic life and "connectivity" today has turned our society a complete one hundred and eighty degrees. We have started to take for granted the most straightforward and efficient tools for communication and replaced them with devices that we THINK are doing a better job for us. In reality people today are more closed off than they ever were and that is unfortunate. Modernization and technology have robbed us of our most core competencies, and we need to claim it back!

The Intricate Things We ARE Deprived Of:

The gatherings with friends and family

The lack of fun festivities

The missing social events

The community spirit and comradery with our peers.

The treatment of everyone around you with respect and dignity that you wish you received.

The Communication with our neighbors.

Possible Causes

There are many possible reasons for this silence struck pandemic. Most of it can be attributed to one or more of the many technological advances that we have seen over the years. No one person has been able to pinpoint exactly what it is that has changed the friendly ways of the world. Here are some of the possible causes. You can try to decide for yourself what you think has been the downfall of communication.

> The Telephone: The invention of the phone made it easier to take the human element out of a conversation. Instead of going to someone's house every so often and staying a few hours, and having a meal, they could call to say what needed to be said, and then cut the conversation short with the excuse that they were wracking up too many minutes that month. They didn't

have to stay on the phone yacking for hours on end because the person on the other end of the line agreed and hung up as well.

The telephone, back when it was invented, was so expensive that only the rich people and government agencies owned them. Created in 1876 by Alexander Graham-Bell, it was the most technologically advanced thing since the dawn of electricity. In the beginning, it cost over a thousand dollars to own a single phone. To make a call, Bell Telephone Industries charged a dollar a minute to dispatch that call. That was a lot of money considering the average worker was lucky to make fifty cents an hour. One minute call time would have been two hours wages, so most average salary households did not have a telephone in the house. That was until the early 1900's after Henry Ford invented the concept of mass production. A company made a telephone that was way cheaper than Bell Industries old phone design, and they found a better way to dispatch calls to make the calls cheaper. During this time, wages went up a lot as well. By this period the minimum wage was about two dollars an hour. This made phones more common in average households. By the nineteen seventies, a home phone was a staple in each house and calls only cost ten cents a minute. This was a great thing, as, by this time, wages were up to seven dollars an hour for minimum wage. The company that was instrumental in lowering the price of the phone? Well, these days it's known as AT&T.

Due to its cost, the telephone may not have been the downfall of modern communication, but it definitely could have had a hand in it. Particularly as it became easier, and cheaper to purchase. People called rather than stopped by, and these calls did not have to drone on and on, as time was money. This allowed conversations to become shorter, and it made its way into everyday life as well.

Television: The television was a lot cheaper than the telephone was. It was also a way to get the news a lot easier, as you didn't have to wait until a friend heard something and get back to you. There were also some good programs to watch during the day that entertained people. This entertainment made them want to stay inside and watch it all day. Well, the adults at least. Children were still sent outside to play.

The original television was black and white and only had three channels. It was small and could sit on the dining room table. Brand new, they cost about three hundred dollars, and they had long rabbit ear antennas. In the beginning, this was the only option you had, but as time went on, there were bigger console televisions available. Eventually, the color television was introduced, and some time after that, more channels were added, as cable became a thing. More and more time was spent inside watching TV. Not just by adults anymore, either. Children were inside more often and watched shows that were geared towards their age groups. People went out and mingled with their neighbors less and less.

Television alone probably was not the downfall of the communication era, but it was a precedent to it. A lot of people began staying inside to watch their soaps instead of going outside to spend time with actual people. For the longest time, children were still sent out to play while the parents watched TV, but as the parents moved to colored cable, the children got the still working black and white rabbit-eared television, and the trend progressed as in the older days, television sets lasted forever.

Game Consoles: Today there are several hi-tech game consoles out there for people to choose from, and they are often played for hours on end, while the player ignores the outside world. Back when they were first invented, they were a lot different, but no less desirable. They were the envy of every household, and a child that had one was instantly familiar, but he never used that popularity because he was too busy inside playing his new game. When the original Atari came out, it was the sensation that swept the nation.

The first ever game console was nothing like the ones we have today. They took a lot more effort to play. To make a single move, you had to write a program first. This was difficult, but the kids in those days didn't mind, as to them it was a game console, and that was the coolest thing they had ever seen. They also learned about computer programming before home computers were a thing. As time progressed, the programs were written into the game at production, so all kids had to do was play the game. They also went from almost fifteen hundred dollars to a hundred and fifty dollars. While that was still pretty expensive, it was a lot more affordable than the Atari. The most popular and innovative of these new consoles? The Nintendo Entertainment System, or NES for short. It was the console that every kid wanted, and most kids were able to get for Christmas or their birthday. With the debut of the game Super Mario Brothers stepping away from the typical games of Pong and Galactica, this thrilling console had kids of all ages, and even adults gathered around it to enjoy it. This further engulfed them into their anti-social bubbles as they were too engrossed in the games to go outside.

Video Games are blamed by many as being the downfall of modern society. That can be seen as accurate, as there were so many people beginning to stay indoors rather than going outside. However, there were plenty of friendly people left in the world, and people still visited one another, so is this the truth? Maybe as they progressed, but it was not an immediate destruction.

Media: This one can be brutal. People are so easily influenced by the media, that they could tell the people that Donald Trump farted unicorns, and they would almost believe it. Okay, maybe not that sorry, but that is the general idea with the media. Nowadays, the media is filled with bombings, kidnappings and other fear mongering materials that it makes it hard to trust the people around you.

In the beginning, the news just stated that. The news. It gave news of the war if there was one, and news With all the fear-inducing news, it makes it hard to want to even talk to anyone, because it seems as if everyone is a murderer now. This is not a conducive environment like friendly ways of the past.

Media could be considered the downfall of the friendly atmosphere, as it seeds fear of the human race in your mind, and that is what seems to have closed people off from their natural chatty instincts.

Internet: The dawn of the web saw a rise in introverts massively. It is no secret that the web has taken over the minds of most of our youth. This goes hand in hand with the media, as it is the primary source of all media output.

So those are some of the possible causes of why it is harder now to talk to people than it used to be. Of course, for some people, it is more difficult than others. Individuals with anxiety or shyness have a hard time even talking to people that are deemed safe by people they trust. It isn't caused by fear, just a nervousness that causes these people to clam up. Chances are since you are reading this, you are one of these people.

Do not fret. This book will help you get through this. However, be prepared. Sometimes it takes more than self-help, and if your problem has deeper seated issues, you may want to get the help of a psychiatrist. If these tips do not help, it is best to seek the help of one if you wish to be more of a conversationalist, and it is essential for your mental and emotional health. There will be more on that at the end of this book.

Chapter 2

Conversation Tips

Step One-Talking to Yourself

This may seem a little silly, but it does help. It is the easiest way to get over your shyness, as it is more awkward to talk to yourself than it is to talk to other people. You just have to get past the first hump of not wanting to look like a fool and own it.

Go into a room with a mirror, start by offering your hand to shake and mime shaking hands with the person staring back at you while introducing yourself. This may feel a little weird, as there is not going to be a meeting of hands, due to you only having the conversation with yourself.

Once you get past the standard greeting, it is time to hold a conversation. You can either say your mirrored self's responses, or you can keep them in your head. This is where it can get tricky. You cannot think of specific to you answers, rather, you have to think of general answers, as you are not the person you are talking to. Talk away as if an actual person was holding a conversation with you. You can think of this as a live diary, but more civilized and social, as you don't want to spill your secrets to someone who is mostly standing in as a stranger.

Here is a little scenario to help you visualize what it would be like.

SCENARIO

Kelly had just finished reading *How to Talk to Anyone: Ten Secrets You Wish You Knew*, and she wanted to try out the first tip, which was called "Talking to Yourself." She stepped into her bathroom and closed the door.

"Okay, Kelly. You can do this. You have to become better at holding a conversation, as your husband's job requires you to attend various social events with him."

Looking into the mirror she offered her hand to the cold glass, feeling slightly foolish.

"Hello, my name is Kelly. And you are?"

In her head, she planned the response.

I am Richard Simms. A pleasure to meet you, Kelly. She used her husband's boss's name as that was the one she was sure she knew.

"Pleasure to meet you too, sir. How are you and your wife and kids?"

They are doing well, as am I. How about your children?

"Oh, no children yet sir. Wanting to get ahead financially first."

A great plan, I must say. Children are very expensive little buggers.

Kelly was interrupted then, as her husband walked into the bathroom.

"Who on Earth are you talking to?"

"I am practicing holding a conversation. I don't want to embarrass you tomorrow at the banquet." Kelly blushed.

"Awe, sweetheart, you could never embarrass me, but I appreciate the effort, and I am glad you are taking the steps necessary to better yourself. I am proud of you." Her husband kissed her forehead and left.

After that boost of confidence, Kelly found it much easier to practice her conversation skills and felt less awkward about talking to herself in the mirror.

It may seem embarrassing to talk to yourself in a mirror, but after awhile it will be much easier, as you will start to feel better about helping yourself become the best that you can be. If someone comes in and asks you what you are doing, explain to them what you are trying to do. You never know, maybe they will try it for themselves.

Of course, there is still a stigma that talking to yourself means that you are crazy, but once you explain that you are not trying to be weird, you just are trying to become better at conversation, people will understand. It is getting harder and harder for people to hold a normal conversation in this world, so it is always refreshing to hear that someone is trying to better themselves.

Step Two- Have a Few Ice Breakers

It is no secret that after the initial introductions conversation gets awkward if there are no real conversation starters in the room. You say hello, state your name, and ask a few questions about what the person does, and how their day has been, but after that is over, this is when the conversation dies out with a bunch of "Ums" and "Uhhh." Having a few icebreakers is always important as you can keep the conversation going, and often have a few laughs going at the end.

Of course, it is hard to tell exactly what you should use as an icebreaker, and that is why most people have a hard time keeping the conversation going. However, few foolproof icebreakers will make talking to someone a breeze. This section will go over some ice breakers to use... and some to avoid.

Real Ice Breakers

> Latest viral cat video: Pretty much everyone in the world loves cat videos, and a lot of people have seen them. Bringing that up in conversation is always a good way of push conversation along. It is a safe topic that won't offend people, and if someone hasn't seen the video, you can show it to them, eliciting a few laughs and smiles. Almost everyone loves cat videos.
>
> Food: Everyone eats. So ask the person what kind of food they like. It is always pertinent to ask them first because if they are vegan, you don't want to say "Bacon is the greatest, is it not?" Discuss different cuisines, and if they have not tried one of your favorites, suggest a good place find it. Talking about food can bring people closer together, as they find common likes and interests in cuisines.

Music: Everyone listens to music. No matter what their tastes, everyone loves music. You cannot deny the fact that life would be boring without it. It fills the awkward silences, and it can bring up someone who is down. There is no escaping the fact that music is tied to emotions as well. Try asking the person what their favorite song is. Ask them the genres they like. If you find you have some interests that are similar, that is great, and that will further boost the conversation.

Hobbies: Everyone has a passion that probably has nothing to do with their job. Hobbies are what make life interesting. It is a safe topic to approach because many people love to talk about what they enjoy, but rarely anyone asks.

Anything to do with interests: Pretty much anything to do with personal interests is safe to talk about because people love to talk about themselves. They like to make known what they enjoy, and they love when someone shows interest in them. However, most people are too shy to talk about themselves unprompted because they do not wish to seem conceited.

Bad Ice Breakers

Politics: There are so many different opinions out there, and unfortunately with the policy, everyone thinks that they are right. The conversation can get awkward if you are a Democrat butting heads with a Republican. That is only the tip of the iceberg though. Tempers often flare at the slightest mention that either party may be corrupt, so it is best all around to just avoid the conversation entirely.

Religion: This is another one that is best avoided. Religion is a very sensitive subject for some, and no one wants someone else's religion shoved in their faces. That is why you are better off keeping this one put away.

Life choices: It is great that you have decided to become a vegan and all, but you do not have to convert everyone who is around you. Same with any of the life choices you make, whether you sell Avon or those scammy weight loss products, virtually no one wants to hear the spiel. Save it for if you are asked.

So there you have it. Some good and some not-so-good icebreakers to help you extend any conversation past the initial hello. Once you can establish a gateway to the conversation, you will be able to carry on a lot easier than you would if you had not used an icebreaker at all, and were floundering about like a fish out of water, trying to figure out what to say.

How These Tips Help

These tips help you relax a little bit. They give you a little confidence boost, knowing that you are prepared to hold a conversation with people you may meet because you have practiced the basics. It is a lot easier to do something once you have practiced it a few times.

It also helps you get past the awkwardness, as nothing is more awkward than holding a conversation with yourself. You will be able to talk to someone without feeling silly because you couldn't possibly feel any goofier than you did speak to a mirror.

Follow these tips to get the ball rolling on talking to people.

Chapter 3

Holding a Conversation

Now that you have gotten past the tips on how to approach and talk to someone, it is time to move on to the advice on how to hold a conversation. This is important because starting a conversation is only a small part of the battle. This means that you have to be able to continue a conversation past the point of the icebreaker.

Conversations do not have to be hours long, but you do have to keep them at a length that does not make you seem rude, or disinterested. If you only talk to someone about one subject and then leave, the person will feel as if they did something to offend you or something like that. You do not want to leave anyone feeling that way.

The best way to avoid that is to make sure that you keep the conversation going to the point where it would be safe to exit without offending the person you are talking too. This section will help you more understand how to keep a conversation going and keep it going well.

Tip Three- Self Disclosure

To understand this advice, there is going to have to be some in-depth explanation of what self-disclosure is. To save you from having to look it up, this tip will include all the information you need to know about it. Of course, that will make this trip a lot longer, but it is better to have a long tip that you understand than a short briefing on something that leaves you confused.

Self-disclosure is where you add to a conversation by giving the other person information about yourself. This is a hard thing to do, as most people worry about boring others with talk of themselves, or they are afraid to seem conceited.

There are two dimensions to self-disclosure. They are breadth and depth. These are both essential to holding a good conversation, and connecting with the person you are talking to. You want to be able to connect with the people around you or else you will not be able to hold a genuine and meaningful conversation. You have to have both to enable the act of self-disclosure indeed.

The breadth of self-disclosure refers to the range of topics you discuss when opening up about yourself. No, you don't have to disclose your deepest darkest secrets, but giving someone a little bit of information about several different subjects about yourself allows them to feel a little closer to you, thus enabling them to open up about themselves. This helps extend the conversation and lets the person feel values as if you are interested in talking with them. Try starting with the easiest topics, such as interests, and move on to schooling, and views on the world. The more subjects you cover, the longer the conversation will be, and the more you will be able to connect with the person you are talking too.

Depth is slightly harder to reach. Now if you are just chatting up with someone you don't plan to develop a deep friendship with, you can almost skip depth, but a deep conversation is necessary for those you wish to establish a real friendship with. However, even in a simple conversation, you need to have some depth to what you are saying. Tell them about the time you broke your arm in third grade, or something of the like. Give them a memory to make them feel as if you care about the conversation you are having, and are not just chatting to pass the time.

The act of self-disclosure is a type of social penetration. This is a theory that you can only establish any relationship, whether it be romantic or platonic, by communication. But not just any type of communication, systematically fluid conversation. This means that over time, you let the person in more and more, and you change the direction of your conversation regularly to establish a connection with the individual you are communicating with.

You also have to allow time for the person to reciprocate in the conversation. Don't spend the entire time talking about yourself. If you are worried about droning on too long about what you like and such, try employing the one detail method.

This means that you share a detail about yourself, and let the other person share a detail about themselves. Continue this on until you find a happy medium between not sharing enough and talking too much.

As you can see self-disclosure is critical, as you need to allow, a person to feel as if you are invested in the conversation. If you do not seem like you care to talk to them, they will close off, and not want to talk much more than the basic hello followed by an icebreaker subject. So how do you efficiently employ this technique?

>Start Small: On top of them feeling like you are interested, they also have to be interested in what you have to say. Rather than unloading a whole pile of information on someone that doesn't care, start with a small bit of information to see if they take the bait. If you use the icebreaker about music, try telling them your favorite song, and explaining a final reason for why you love it. If they just give you a one-word reply, it is best to duck out of the conversation then. They

don't care. However, if they seem interested, and ask you, more then you can start talking about more of your interests and such.

Decide on The Type of Conversation: You should always try to approach every conversation as if you seek to make a new friend. However, if you are at a convention with people from around the globe, chances are you are not going to establish a life-long friendship. You should still show interest in the individual, but that would impact the type of information that you are going to divulge. You don't want someone you are never going to see again knowing a deep secret about you. Instead, tell them about childhood memories that you don't feel would impact how they think of you. Your favorite thing to do as a child or stuff like that. Those are safe subjects for people who you are just talking to at that moment.

Skim the Surface: You want people to be interested in you for a long time. This means that you cannot divulge everything about you in one conversation. You have to be conservative with your information. The best way to do this is to take a little bit of information from many different subjects to talk about. As you get to know a person more and more, you can add more details to that. This helps you also ensure that you are not talking about yourself too much.

Allow Reciprocation: The best part of self-disclosure is that it allows the other person a gateway to say themselves as well. You don't want to hog the stage and only talk about yourself. You want to keep the flow of information even. Give the other person some time to tell you about themselves as well. The conversation will come alight as you are swapping stories and some fun little tidbits of information about yourself.

Be Loose: Telling someone about yourself should be done with ease. You don't want to sound like someone who is selling something, though in reality that is what you are doing in a way. You are trying to convince the person to like you with the truth. However, it should not sound like you are a documentary. You should be light and airy when talking about yourself. Make the person interested. Intrigue them, and draw them in, get them want to know more about you.

Timing: Just like when you deliver the punchline to a joke, it is all about the timing. You have to time the information that you provide. This is a little tricky if you don't know what goes into timing a deliverance. There has to be a level of interest from the other person. To ensure that you have their interest, you have to make them ask a few questions. You can't just offer up all the information. However, you can't make them pry every bit of info from you either. There has to be a give and take kind of flow going on there.

Caution: There are some things that you do not tell a person you just met. It may seem like you have known the person forever, but you still have to use caution when divulging certain things. For example, if you were a former addict, it is best not to mention it unless necessary. You do not want anything to skew how they think of you until they get to know you. If you are confident in yourself, however, then try divulging that info. What you are cautious with depends on you.

There you have it. Self-disclosure at its finest. This is one of the most important things to holding a good conversation. Now, remember, your entire conversation does not have to consist of self-disclosure alone, but throwing in a few facts here and there go a long way. Make sure you utilize this to the fullest advantage possible.

Tip Four- Engage the Other Person Fully

Part of the problem these days is that conversation becomes one sided. Even though both parties are speaking, they are not really in the conversation. They are not properly engaging the other person. This is a big issue when communication relies entirely on both parties being actively involved in the discussion to allow it to succeed. If you are not actively engaging the other person, and not participating yourself, then you will fall flat in the conversation.

First off, how you can be engaged in the conversation better, without taking it over.

> Actively Listen: No one wants to feel like they are talking to a brick wall. They want to feel like the person they are talking to is genuinely interested in what they have to say. This means that you have to listen to understand. Today's generation teaches you to hear the reply, and that is where the problem lies. By only looking to respond, you are not processing what the other person is saying because your mind is on yourself. This is a selfish, bad habit that this day and age has taken to sticking too.

> Reply with Interest: Even if you are not quite interested in what the other person is talking about, you should always respond with interest. It is polite, and even though you may not be interested in it now, you might gain some interesting knowledge by listening to what they have to say. You can't just

expect everyone to have the same interests as you, and there are probably things that you like that others do not like but they still act like they are at least interested in it, because it is the polite thing to do.

Ask Questions: Asking questions to get more information about what they are talking about shows the other person that you were listening, and that you want to know more. It allows the person to be relieved because then they do not feel like they are boring you with their information. The only way that they know that you are interested is if you are asking questions. Then they know that it is okay to continue talking about the subject they are on.

Be THERE: I know it can be hard if someone is droning on and on about something that you have no interest in, but it is still good etiquette to be there mentally. This means that when someone is talking, don't let your mind go on vacation, and tune the person out because if you are that disinterested in them, it is more polite to change the subject rather than just leave the conversation mentally.

That is how you can be engaged in a conversation. Following these tips will allow you to breathe easier knowing that you are pleasantly talking to a person, and you won't offend them because you seem disinterested. You just have to practice these things, because sometimes it can be a little tricky.

How to Engage Them

>Be Interesting: This does not mean you have to make up stories. It has nothing to do with the information you are giving at all. You just have to deliver it in an interesting way. You could tell someone you climbed Mount Everest on the back of Dwayne Johnson, and if you inform the story in a monotone voice, it will sound dull. It is not what you are saying; it is how you are saying. Tell them your stories as if you were telling them for the first time. Be engaged yourself, and show the person that you want them to talk to you. You

want their attention. Only then will you get the attention you so desire.

Leave Openings: Even without using self-disclosure, you still have to leave openings for the other person to talk, no matter the subject. No one wants to stand there and listen to someone take control of the conversation. You might as well be talking to yourself for that matter. Or to the plant in the corner. You have to let the other person talk as well. A good conversation allows both parties to talk equally and without any hitches. It is not people talking about everything while the other person stands there and nods.

Allow Questions: If a person asks a question, don't dodge it. This should not have to be said, but a lot of people avoid questions for fear of sounding conceited, but in truth, you just seem rude. If someone is asking a question, you are not going to sound pretentious by answering it. If you dodge a question, the person will feel as if they offended you, and they will be less likely to stay engaged in the conversation.

That is how you engage someone in conversation. It is a lot easier than staying involved in a discussion as long as they are interested in what is being said. All you have to do is be open and friendly, and let the rest fall into place.

How These Tips Help

These tips are designed to help you keep a conversation going without being nervous. These tips also contribute to improving your communication skills. By using these tips, you will feel more comfortable having a longer conversation with someone that you just met than you would be if you were just trying to find things to talk about.

These tips will give you the boost you need to feel confident in your abilities to talk to people and enjoy the conversation without having to worry every second that you are saying something wrong.

Chapter 4

Getting Through a Conversation

These tips are for what you should do during and after a conversation with someone. They are tips on how to properly act when communicating, as there is often some confusion about what to do especially now that it is no longer a curriculum at school or home. Do not fret. This book will clarify that right up.

Tip Five- Etiquette During a Conversation

It is of utmost importance that you have the proper etiquette when talking to someone. The key to holding a good conversation is not to offend them and to show them that you are a real person to talk to. You want to keep their attention and let them know that they have yours. Otherwise, you will not get very far in the communication realm, as people will not want to talk to you, thinking you are rude.

So it is best to study up on proper etiquette before you put yourself out there. While most of these are common sense, they are in here just in case nerves cause a problem with combining common sense with communication. That is a real issue a lot of people have. They cannot rely on their common sense because they are too nervous to remember to use it.

So here are the etiquette rules to help you out. Remember, a slip up is okay as long as you don't do it continually, but it is best to try to be as clean cut as possible to avoid any issues.

> Handshake: This is the first thing you should do, as you say hello. Unless the person is germaphobic, or you are, not offering a handshake is considered rude. If you do have a phobia of germs, it is best to explain that as you are saying hello, so there are no misunderstandings. Make sure that they know that you are still pleased to meet them; you just would rather not shake their hand. Most people can be pretty understanding.
>
> The perfect handshake is firm but pliant. You can't grip too tight, because you are not trying to intimidate someone, and a grip too loose makes people feel that

you are not that thrilled to meet them, and are only doing so out of necessity. This is not a great first impression, as people want to feel like they are worth getting to know. So it is best to make sure you give a real, genuine handshake.

Eye Contact: This one is important to maintain from the beginning to end. It is always disconcerting to talk to someone who is looking off into the distance or anywhere else but who is talking to them. (autistic people are not counted in this, nor are the ocularly impaired) Eye contact shows that you are paying attention to them. To show you why eye contact is so important, let us have a mini history lesson.

Back in the time of extreme social hierarchy, where people who made less money than you were deemed undesirable, eye contact was a way of establishing that social ladder. Anyone who was considered below you had to make eye contact with you, while you were not to make eye contact with them. To make eye contact with a person deemed lowly, put you on their level, and could cause you to lose your social position if caught.

Kings never looked anyone but other kings in the eye, no one ever made eye contact with serfs other than other serfs. Men did not make eye contact with women, as even women were deemed below them. They only time someone made eye contact with a lady that was not another woman, was a servant, or a peasant to a duchess or queen. Eye contact was the primary factor of social hierarchy

By not looking someone in the eye during a conversation, you are essentially saying that they are beneath you and that what they have to say is n't matter. That may not be what you are trying to do, but that is the message you are portraying when you refuse to look someone in the eye.

> Body Language: This will be more brushed on in a later chapter, but it also falls under etiquette. You have to have an open body language in a conversation.

Otherwise, you risk making a person feel as if you are unapproachable, and not open to discussion. You can also make them feel as if what they are saying has no value. You can do so much damage with a few simple gestures, and this is a problem. You have to be careful with your stance and make sure that you are not closing yourself off.

No Phone: This should go without saying, but if your phone goes off, DON'T ANSWER IT! Society today is so caught up in the conversations that they have going on on the other side of the screen, that they forget the importance of conversation with the person on the other aspect of the table. You are in a real time conversation with a real person. (Not that the person texting you isn't real, but they are not there.) The best thing to do is to put your phone on silent if you know you are going to talk to people. That way you do not feel tempted to pull it out and text rather than speaking with those around you.

Cell phones are a wonderfully destructive device. They can help you connect with people from around the world, but unfortunately, that causes you to disconnect from the people that are right next to you. A lot of people use their phone as a crutch to not have to talk to people when they feel uncomfortable. This does not help you in any way. They only way to become comfortable with a situation is to put yourself out there and talk to people. Find someone to talk to and eventually you will take your mind off of the fact that you are anxious about being around people.

Don't Interrupt: When someone is talking to you, it is best to stay quiet until you are sure they have finished what they are saying. You have to be very careful when talking to someone that you are listening to them, and not listening to respond. This is one of the biggest problems in today's conversations. No one looks to people for more than knowing when to jump in and reply. This leads to more people interrupting, which often angers the other person, and makes them not want to talk to you any longer.

Listen to the person, and remember that you would not want to be interrupted. No one likes to be talked over, and no one likes talking to someone who constantly does it. Be patient. Your time to talk will come.

Personal Space: This is a big one. A lot of people get really close to people when they are talking. This is uncomfortable for the other person. You have to make sure that you keep a safe distance between you and the other person. Arm's length apart is a good chatting distance unless you are in a loud place, and then from forearm length apart is usually as close as you should be. If it is too loud to hear, then you should hold the conversation until you are in a quieter environment.

Claustrophobia is a big problem for a vast majority of a population. Invading someone's personal space can make them very uncomfortable. You have to respect that people need personal space when talking to you.

Even if they don't have claustrophobia, it is still gross when someone is so close to you that you can feel their spit as they are talking. Keep the distance.

Get Close: This may seem to contradict the last statement, but you have to be close enough that it does not look like you are trying to escape the conversation. However, it is not that contradictory. You just have to find a happy medium. You want to be close enough that the other person is not sniffing themselves trying to figure out if it is them, but you have to be far enough away that you are not crowding their personal space.

A good indicator is your arms. Of course, you do not physically stretch them out to see if you are standing close enough, but rather you visualize where you are at. You should never be so close that you have to bend your arm at more than a ninety-degree angle to touch them, but you should not be so far away that when your arms are fully outstretched your palms can't rest on their shoulders. Try to stay in that golden circle of space, and you should be good.

Those are the tips for etiquette during a conversation. Follow these, and you should have no problem with people not wanting to talk to you. You will make the other person feel respected, and that is what you are striving for.

Tip Six- Etiquette When Leaving a Conversation

Timing: As stated before, timing is everything when talking to people. You have to be good at your timing and actually, know when to say something when not to say something. In this case, timing has to do with when to exit a conversation. No matter how good a conversation has been, you begin to wear out your welcome. If a person starts to look around or shift about, they are probably ready to go or do something else. This is your cue to end the conversation if they do not. Finish what you were saying, and then use an exit phrase such as "Oh I can't believe how much of your time I have taken! It was so great talking to you I just got swept up at the moment!" Make them feel good while ending the conversation.

Ending Phrase: As mentioned in the above bullet, you have to use a good ending phrase to make the person feel as if the conversation end is not their fault, even if it is. Be polite, and make them feel like you were so enthralled by talking to them that you regret having to end the conversation, but you do not want to take up any more of their time. This will make them feel valued, and that will get them want to talk to you again.

Ask for Contact Info: If you have the chance of seeing someone again, or just would like to stay in touch, ask if they would like to exchange contact information. If they say yes, go ahead and give them your number and ask for theirs, giving a test call to make sure you input the number right and allowing them to be sure of the same, as the will have your number on the call. If they do not wish to exchange information, do not push. It doesn't mean you did anything wrong; they just may not think that they will see you again. That is okay.

Always ask if they want to exchange information. It is a lot more comfortable for them, as it gives them a little more room to say no without feeling bad. Asking them for their contact information directly does not allow for them to say no without feeling bad because you assumed that they wanted to. Remember, the right conversation does not mean they have to become your best friend. A lot of people get so attached to someone they had a single enthralling conversation with, that they are upset when the person does not want to keep in touch. This is only human nature, as we are designed to communicate for survival. Breaking yourself of this habit will be difficult, but if you do it, you will be less affected by the rejection you feel when someone does not wish to stay in touch.

> Follow Up: This only refers to people who exchanged info. If they give you their contact information, then

text or call them the next day to see how they are doing and let them know that you were serious about wanting to stay in touch. Make the person feel important, but only text once, and let them respond. They might be busy when you try to reach them and will get back to you later.

These are the etiquette rules for ending a conversation. If you use them, you can be confident that you are not leaving someone with awkwardness in the air.

How These Tips Help

These tips give you the boost up in a conversation to show a person that you are respectful, and that you have proper manners. This will make them enjoy talking to you a lot better than if you did not know these rules.

Etiquette is slowly slipping away, by trying to bring it back, you will also start a ripple effect, as the person you are talking to will pick up on these social cues, and start using them in their conversations with others. By doing this little simple thing, you can help bring proper communication etiquette back into a trend.

Chapter 5

Additional Tips

These tips are just extra tips that you should know and insert throughout different conversations. They do not necessarily have to apply to every conversation, as they are not about the conversation itself, but how to psych yourself up to talk to people, and how to handle rejection without letting it ruin you.

Tip Seven- Get Out of Your Head

You have to get out of your own head to ever hold a good conversation with someone because you have to be able to approach someone to talk to them. If you are stuck in your head, and the "Oh I can't" thoughts, then you will be stuck at only talking to people you have to.

By getting out of your head, you will feel confident enough to approach a person that you have never met before, and that has no correlation to any of your friends. This is the best feeling, knowing that you can make friends anywhere, and not have to worry about going somewhere and not knowing anyone there.

Imagine you are going to a party. Your friend says that they will meet you there. You are glad, because you don't know anyone else who will be attending, or they are just minor acquaintances from work or school. You get there, and your friend texts you were saying that they can't come because something came up. You don't panic because you decide just to go find someone to talk to. You walk up to a guy or girl you have never seen before and strike up a conversation. Before the night is up, you have met seven new people that you really get along with.

That is what can happen once you stop the thoughts that you aren't good enough to talk to someone, or that you are too boring for anyone to want to talk to. Confidence is key. Boost yourself up, and as they say, fake it till you make it. You have to boost yourself up because there is not going to be anyone in the world who is able to make you feel better about yourself than you can. Go in with the mindset that you are worth talking to, and that you are funny and witty. By believing in yourself, people will be more open to you, as they can see that you are confident in yourself.

Tip Eight- Boost Your Self Esteem

This one goes hand in hand with getting out of your head. You have to believe in yourself to get out of your head. If you have low self-esteem, you will be more prone to rejection, because just like lions, people can pick out the ugly ones. No one wants to have to carry the entire conversation, so they generally steer away from the shy people, and gravitate to someone who they know will actively engage in conversation.

The way to boost your self-esteem can also involve a mirror. Stand in front of it for ten minutes a day only saying positive things about yourself. You are smart; you are strong, you are caring, you are kind. Do not mention any of your negative attributes. For every negative thing you say, add another minute to the time you spend looking in the mirror. It is your responsibility to build yourself up, no one else's. You can do it. As the days go on, you will find you are having to add less time onto your ten minutes, until finally, you spend just the ten minutes saying entirely positive things about yourself. Eventually, you will begin to believe them. You are essentially retraining your brain to say nice things to you, rather than mean things.

This society is so bleak, and some so many mean people say hateful things while hiding behind a computer screen, and this has cause self-esteem rates to go way down. Build yourself back up to stay above the hatred

Tip Nine- Handle Rejection with Pride

If you have low self-esteem, this will be hard, so you have to build yourself up to be able to do this. Otherwise, it will get to you, and make you not want to talk to people any longer. If you are rejected before you build yourself up, just take some time to recuperate.

Not everyone will want to talk to you, especially nowadays. In today's age, people judge others before they even open their mouths, and decide on if a person is "worthy" of speaking to them. You have to break away from this thinking. You also cannot think that someone is above your level, they may seem like they are, and turn out to be the nicest person ever. However, when you approach someone, they may reject you, and this is okay. You may not want to talk to anyone that approaches you either.

If you are rejected, shake it off. Remind yourself that it is not you, it is who they are. They decided that they did not want to get to know you, and that is their loss, not yours. Get back up on that metaphorical horse and try again with someone else. You will find someone who is actually worth talking to.

Tip Ten- Don't Latch On

In a setting with a lot of people, it is so easy to try to find people that you enjoy talking to and staying with them a majority of the time. This is not a superb idea. You have to work for the crowd so to speak. How boring would it be if you were at a concert, and the singer only interacted with one fan? It is the same concept with talking to people. Go around to different people, and try to make more than one new friend. Eventually, you can come back to that one person, but let them have some time to talk to others, and give yourself time to talk to others as well.

How These Tips Help

These tips are for your own personal use to adapt to specific conversations and situation, and to psych yourself up before you go to a social event where you may not know someone that is there.

Following these tips will give you an edge on your conversations. Using these will help give you a self-esteem boost, and you will learn how to help yourself. These tips will make you a better conversationalist and a better you.

Chapter 6

After the Tips

If you have tried all of these tips, and find that you still cannot connect with people, you should try to see about getting some help with a psychiatrist. There could be some real deep-seated issues there. Talking to people is hard, but if you have tried to break out of your shell, and find yourself having panic attacks every time, you need to know what is going wrong.

There is nothing wrong with getting help either. Just as you would need to see a doctor for a physical illness, you should see a psychiatrist if your social anxiety is so bad that it is causing you to break down at the thought of talking to someone you do not know. There are a lot of resources that are at your disposal. If you are not sure a psychiatrist in your area, try talking to your average doctor, and he can help refer you to someone. The best thing about that is he is more likely to know a specialist to ensure that you are getting the best level of help that you can get.

How to know if it is more than just being shy

> You have panic attacks regularly in social situations: This can be the sign of a serious problem. You should get it checked out, and maybe the doctor can help you figure out how to work through it in a way that is best suited to you.

You avoid stores during busy hours: If you would rather go without a necessity for a period of time because you do not want to visit a store during working hours as there will be too many people there, and could cause you to have a meltdown, you should see a doctor. This is serious. You cannot deny your needs. A physician can help you figure out the root of the problem, and set you on your way to healing.

> If you feel physically ill in social situations where there are only a handful of people: If being in small groups makes you feel physically ill, you should definitely look

into it. Doing so allows you to truly live your life to the fullest, once you figure out what is wrong.

Don't let anxiety control your life any longer. Get the help you deserve and do not feel bad for doing so. You deserve to live a happy life unrestrained by anxiety. Regain control of your life.

PART IV

CHAPTER 1

FIVE KEYS TO FIRE UP

Before presenting the Five Keys to reignite the fire in your relationship, we wanted you to know that you are not the only one, or only couple, to have issues when it comes to losing your initial passion. Recent studies tell the real story: More than 1/3 of women between the ages of 18 to 59 years old suffer from a lack of desire for sex (1). Women are not the only ones experiencing problems in their sex lives. Sixty-two percent of men today say no to sex more frequently than women (2). We've lost our drive! It's not that most of can't enjoy sex or can't perform, it's that most of us just don't want to have sex. Perhaps the sex we've been having hasn't left us wanting more of the same.

Of course, a decrease in your sex drive can be caused by a number of medical reasons, such as depression, high blood pressure, medications, increased stress hormones, and low testosterone levels, among other things. Or, decreased sex drives can be correlated to low energy levels, over-crowded schedules, family distractions, abusive backgrounds, or poor past experiences with sex. Some with medical issues or deep emotional scars may need to consult with a professional sex therapist or physician to regain healthy functioning.

The first thing you need to do is admit you have a sexual problem. No, you don't have to go to a meeting, introduce yourself to the group, and tell them all about your sexual dysfunction. Although I'm sure there's an encounter group for that, as well. It might be less stressful and more enlightening to examine some of the things that could be causing your low libido. Keep in mind, the reasons for a decreased sex drive can be much different between men and women.

Why Is There No Fire in Your Relationship?

To many women, sex seems somewhat unimportant; you might say it's low on their "to-do" list. Women who display these rather lackluster emotions toward sex certainly don't flip the fire switch for their partners. Emotional detachment to sex sucks all the energy out of the act. Many men who lack desire for sex can usually link their doused fire to job-related stress, money worries, and repeated rejection. Having sex then becomes robotic and routine; there just isn't enough return on the emotional or physical investment.

Here are some of the most common reasons both men and women have given for decreases in their sexual desires.

- Fear of being judged or criticized

- No more emotional connection

- Just another chore

- Too many interruptions

- Too much on their mind

- Don't have the energy

- Resentment from sex being used as a commodity

- Not enough tenderness or intimacy

- Boring—they've done it all

- He/she takes me for granted

- No fun

- Feelings of unattractiveness

- They'd rather relax in front of the television

- Unsatisfied with physical appearance

- Painful

- Sex is perceived as wrong or sinful

- Previously abusive relationship

- No foreplay—just hop on, hop off, roll over

- Been too long and now they feel awkward

- Partner never initiates sex (3)

The list of reasons for a decreased sex drive is infinite. Then there's the question of boring sex; you're having sex frequently, but it's not that hot, passionate sex that used to make you want to climb out of your skin. To some degree, that's to be expected. It's not that familiarity breeds contempt—it's more like regular sex with the same person can cause complacency. It's a proven fact that people have an instinctive need for newness. We prefer new cars to ones that have given us great service. We want new clothes over those that are more comfortable. Deep within us, we fantasize about the excitement of new partners. Unfortunately, when a new partner is found, it isn't long before that same old bedfellow "boredom" comes to call.

Some men and women are far too patient, putting up with little to no sex for years. What if it's too late to start a fire in your relationship? Put your mind to rest. It's never too late to become a more excitingly sexual person. Even if you cannot reignite the fire in this relationship, learning these Five Keys can help you to build within yourself, and that will certainly get your partner's attention. There is no list of signs that will tell you when your sex drive is waning—you are already experiencing the one most glaring sign—no sex.

So, what are the Five Keys to reignite the fire in your relationship? We thought you'd never ask!

The Five Keys to Reignite the Fire in Your Relationship

We'll go into greater detail later, but for right now I'll introduce the keys and briefly describe their meaning.

Key #1: Making a Game-Time Decision

If you have known for a long time that your relationship was blowing a bit cold, you have a decision to make. Putting the fire back into a relationship doesn't just happen by accident. To create a fire from embers takes a conscious decision and firm resolve to make it happen.

Key #2: Know & Share Your Turn-ons

Many people don't know what really turns them on because they've never exposed themselves. Not that kind of expose! They've never explored their own bodies to understand what turns them on. Being familiar with your "boiling" points is important to know, and to share with your partner. It's especially important if your turn-ons are a bit out of the norm. We'll examine some of those in a later chapter.

Key #3: Maintain the Mystery

Part of that newness we spoke of earlier comes from the fact that a new partner holds mysteries that have yet to be unfolded. We haven't been privy to their private habits that can be a buzz kill to sexual desire. We don't know their secrets, but we look forward to uncovering each tantalizing detail. For this reason, you need to reserve some things for your mystery treasures—to be unburied by your partner.

Key #4: Change It Up

When considering change, it's necessary to broaden your experiences. About all the sexual changes some people experience is the "I'll be on top this time" sort. This key will show you how to create such change that your partner will be anticipating what's to come every time you plan (and planning is an essential element) to have sex.

Key #5: Connecting On All Sexual Cylinders

This Key teaches you how to be all-in. You'll discover the incredible heat from a fire that's been fueled by employing all the Keys. Once you have a menu of choices and throw in the emotions felt from a bonded partner, you'll feel explosively energetic releases.

We've made some pretty ambitious promises, but let me share with you the reasoning behind this knowledge. There are some biological reasons why these Keys build more passionate lovemaking. No matter what your issues are, learning and practicing these Keys will give you much hotter sexual experiences. However, before you try all these things, you need to rule out a medical condition that could be an underlying, or even primary, issue.

Medical Reasons for a Decrease in Sexual Desire

You would think we'd be over the shame and stigma attached to a decline in sexual drives or having issues with sexual dysfunction. Unfortunately, this is not the case, especially for men. Men identify with their ability to perform, considering themselves to be less of a man if they aren't able to maintain an erection, or if they have little desire for sex. Although the feelings are different for women, they are no less damaging to their chances of having hot sex. Many women freely talk to other women about feeling sexually obligated or about giving their partner's sex to get something they want in exchange. It becomes a standing joke in female circles that so-and-so must be great in bed to have earned that new car or exciting trip. Exchanging sex for treats reduces passionate sex to how you would reward a dog for being obedient.

Before we begin discussing the medical and psychological issues that can put out the flame, let's agree to remove the shame or stigma from any problem you might be having. After all, if you had diabetes or high blood pressure, you wouldn't be ashamed, would you? Once the inferior feelings are forgotten, you can get started on overcoming any medical issues that could be the root cause of your inability to have or enjoy great sex.

Two of the most common medical problems that negatively affect your sex life are diabetes and high blood pressure. Females also have a whole other set of issues with the onset of menopause when their hormones tank and the walls of their vagina become thinner and more easily irritated. Younger women can also have hormonal issues when they are breastfeeding. This, however, is not a complicated fix. Most of the time, with a slight change in hormones, they are back to hot sex.

People who have thyroid problems or issues with chronic depression are also susceptible to lower sex drives. If you have nerve damage brought on by Parkinson's, multiple sclerosis, or have had pelvic surgery, these things can impact your ability to enjoy or want sex (4).

All these issues can be improved or eliminated by consulting with and following the advice of a professional. Let's examine some things you can do to improve your sex drive.

Things You Can Do to Improve Your Sex Drive

1. Get plenty of sleep.

    A study done by the University of Chicago revealed that people who sleep less than five hours a night for an extended period will experience the testosterone levels of someone 15 years older (2).

2. Reduce stress.

Stress hormones like cortisol and adrenalin cause resistance to testosterone. Dr. Malcolm Carruthers, founder of the Centre for Men's Health, says: *"I do believe testosterone deficiency is becoming more common and happening younger. It used to affect mostly men in their 50s, but it's now men in their 40s and even their 30s (2)."*

3. Reduce or eliminate the use of alcohol and drugs.
   It also helps to lay off the cigarettes.

4. Eat well and maintain a healthy weight.
   Carrying additional belly fat can block testosterone.

5. If sex is painful for you, don't always make it about intercourse. Spend more time enjoying the foreplay. Also, try different positions. You may find some more comfortable and less painful than others. It's always a good idea to empty your bladder before sex as well (5).

It's easy to know when to contact a professional. The answer is—right away. Don't wait for years to pass without enjoying great sex. Avoid letting physical issues create emotional stress on you and your partner.

When you've cleared up any medical reasons that may be prohibiting your ability to reignite the fire in your relationship, then it's time to move on to the five most important Keys that can help you put the heat back into your sex life.

CHAPTER 2
SECRET KEY #1

MAKING A GAME-TIME DECISION

Obviously, you have a decision to make. This Key can be the most difficult one used to unlock the secrets to lighting that fire in your relationship. The longer you have let your sex life cool, the more difficult it will be to heat things up. Although the decision will be yours to make, you will need open communications and full cooperation with your partner as well. It's a two-fold issue: (1) making the decision; and (2) getting your partner on board with your plan.

You'll notice I have referred to this process as a "game-time" decision. Let me explain what I mean by that term. A game-time decision is usually one made just at the time of play—at the exact time things need to happen. All the preparation has gone into making the decision, and then it is time to jump in and start the game. That's what it's going to be like to begin using the Keys for improving your sex life. All the preparation in the world isn't going to make that moment you decide to jump in any less awkward or stressful. What it will do is give you the courage and confidence that you are doing the right thing.

So, let's examine all the elements of preparation that will lead up to your game-time decision. You'll need to take into consideration the following points before communicating your plan to your partner.

Prepare for that Game-time Move

Deciding to embrace the Keys to hot sex is no easy endeavor. It's important to consider the elements that make up good decision-making strategies. The success of this plan could mean a rescued relationship. Don't be fooled into believing that hot sex is always spontaneous. That's the Hollywood version, where people are ripping their clothes off as they come through the door. Not that you won't want to try that strategy later on, but let's get you through the awkwardness first. That way you'll be ready to step up your game as you have some success under your belt—literally.

Taking the time to plan your decision to have great sex with your partner won't take the fun out of it, it will turn up the heat. When you've both planned to make your sex exciting, your anticipation will be a huge payoff. So, these are the elements to consider before making your game-time decision.

Uncertainty

Expect, at first, to feel hesitant and uncertain, insecure and uncomfortable. That's what this is all about, to get you out of your comfort zone. If you don't feel these emotions, you haven't created enough change to bring on the heat, to build the fire. Every time couples try new things, every time you get closer to the fire, there's a chance you'll get burned. That's part of the excitement—taking that chance. So, welcome the insecurity and discomfort; it means you are well on your way to having better sex than you've ever experienced.

Complexity

Many factors will come into play during your decision to reignite the fire in your relationship. Often, the factors that you have to consider will play against one another. For example, you will need to set aside time to build the fire. To do that, it may mean a significant change in your personal schedule, or time taken from other activities to devote to sex. Make your decisions with a clear understanding of how one issue will affect others, then prioritize. What is most important? What will have the greatest impact on your relationship? Somedays hot sex is going to take priority. Somedays, maybe not. However, if sex never comes first, if you consider sex as something to do to appease your partner when there's nothing better going on, it will eventually make you not want to play.

Consequences

There are going to be consequences to the decisions you make; every decision has its consequences—some good, some bad. What you need to do is be prepared for those consequences. For example, if you decide to role-play, or incorporate adult toys into your new sexual explorations, your partner may not agree or understand your need. Just beginning to have more sex may be a bit of a shock. So, understand that with each decision to step up your game, there will be some consequences. If you decide to build some fear of discovery into your sex life, the consequence might be that you could get caught. If that consequence isn't real, the fear won't be there.

The more creative you become when you use these Keys, the greater your results will be as well. Your response to these consequences will depend on your perception. How do you view the word consequence? A consequence is not good or bad in itself. It's simply what happens as a result of the decisions you make. All you want to do is be able to reasonably predict the consequences of your decisions. This ability to predict leads us to the next element of decision-making.

Reasonably Predict the Outcome

If you have properly considered all your options and consequences, you should have a reasonable idea of the results of your decision. When it comes time to jump in—to make that game-time decision, you'll be prepared for what could happen. Not to say the unexpected doesn't sometimes throw you a curve ball, but being able to reasonably predict the outcome of your decision will give you the confidence to handle the unexpected.

Being on your game means that you will, at times, have to make more game-time decisions. That's okay, this very first decision to jump in will prepare you for other decisions to come.

Plan Your Approach

Postponing your decision to just "do it" until the perfect time, is the coward's way out, and it's no way to reignite the heat. There is no perfect time. It's a game-time decision; the time is right now. However, how you plan to approach your partner needs some preparation. The reason you need a strategy is that all these things will come into play when communicating your needs with your partner and getting him or her to become a player as well. Building a fiery relationship is a dual effort. You cannot create the heat all by yourself. So, let's discuss how you will approach your partner.

Set the Scene

Discussing your sexual desires with your partner can be quite intimidating, so set the scene. Timing is everything. Don't wait until you're in a heated argument about your partner's inattentiveness or time spent with other people or things to bring up needing to build more fire in your relationship. Doing this will start the process off with a raging, out-of-control fire, and not usually one that lends itself to having great sex. Anger and resentment often act as fire extinguishers. Since you are the one taking the initiative to build this fire, you need to make sure the winds of discontent aren't blowing so hard that it threatens to either put your fire out or level the city. Setting the scene puts you in control.

When you're setting the stage to discuss your sexual needs, create a time and place where your voice will be heard. Make it a time when you have can freely talk about what you want to do for your partner, explaining in sexy detail how you plan to make your partner feel. Remind your lover how things used to be, how hot your sex was when you first met. In fact, bringing up a particularly exciting sexual exchange is an excellent way to get your partner's attention. See what I mean? If properly planned, the conversation alone can be a turn on.

Explore Together

Once you have made yourself vulnerable by sharing what it is you want, get your partner to join in the game. Ask them about their wants and needs. Exploration means sharing the fantasies as well as the practical ideas. During this time of exploration, make it a "no-holds-barred" kind of thing. Anything goes! Keep in mind, you've been planning this for a while, but your partner hasn't. He or she may also be struggling with insecure, uncertain feelings that might surface during your exploration of the possibilities of bringing back the fire. Again, use all your emotions to stimulate and excite one another.

It's strange how our minds and bodies react to the unknown. Most of us fear the unknown. Let me share something with you about fear. The physiological feelings one experiences with fear are the same as one experiences when you exchange a spark of interest with a stranger. When your central nervous system has been awakened, your sexual arousal will follow suit (6). The feelings of fear and arousal within your body are the same. The body doesn't know the difference; so, creating a bit of fear can be used to stimulate you and your partner's physical responses during the conversation you are having.

Now add touch to the equation, and what you have is the beginnings of a fire, my friend. As you are having this conversation, make sure you are sitting close, touching your partner. At first, the touch can be reassuring, and then see where things go from there.

Create A Vision

Decide ahead of time what you want to happen after having this conversation. If you want it to lead to hot sex, make it happen. Jump in! It could be a game-time decision that will depend on all the factors and options you have already considered. The beauty of being a visionary is that having that picture and being able to predict the outcome.

I'm sure you've heard of athletes who imagine their successful throw of a football or see themselves making a perfect trajectory of the basketball to the hoop. That's what I'm talking about. Create a picture in your mind where you want this conversation to go, and then do what it takes to turn that picture into reality. If you want it to lead to hot sex, create the possibility. If you've communicated the fact that you want to use some sex toys or that you would welcome incorporating some hot videos into your sexual activities, then have those things ready and available.

As you are having the conversation with your partner, explaining some of the things you'd like to do, let them know you have those things ready. Perhaps you could even show them what you have in mind as you're talking. All the while you are having this conversation, keep touching and talking. It's like an adult show and tell, don't you think? It won't be a secret to how your partner is responding to your conversation. You'll hear and see the fire grow until the conversation leads to the act.

Be open to where the conversation takes you. If you have set the scene for building a great fire, explored your options with your partner, and helped them to feel the heat by creating a vision through the senses, then enjoy the sex. The worst thing to do is cry or become angry if your partner doesn't respond the way you thought her or she would. Have a screaming match and storming out will make it that much harder to achieve your goal of reigniting the fire in your relationship. You've set yourself up for failure if you sit in your usual TV spots during a football game, agree to turn the sound down but leave the picture on, and clinically talk about your lackluster sex. It's almost a sure thing that after that kind of conversation, you'll have nothing to look forward to but the outcome of the game. If this is how you set the scene, then you've just tried to build your fire in the middle of a torrential downpour. It ain't gonna happen!

Some people decide to use the vision approach first. They set the scene and plan on further exploration by creating an atmosphere of surprise. The story of Tasha and Derrick will illustrate what I mean.

Tasha and Derrick had been dating for five years, and they had both slipped into the comfort and ease of Saturday "honey dos" and Sunday afternoon sports. Their routine was comfortable and pleasant, but they lacked heat in the romantic department. It's not that they didn't have sex, but it always seemed to follow that same easy, comfortable path as the rest of the time they spent together.

Sometimes Derrick and Tasha would decide to watch the football game at the neighbors. If it was a late game, Tasha would sneak out a little early, light up the grill, and have a few burgers or hot dogs ready for dinner when Derrick returned home. This Sunday she decided things were going to be a bit different. Tasha was going to light a fire, but it wasn't going to be for hamburgers. Tasha had made a decision to create some heat in her and Derrick's relationship, and she had planned well ahead of time.

Instead of hamburgers and hotdogs, Derrick came home to a darkened room with burning candles, some large, vibrating toys and an erotic video laying on the coffee table. Next, he saw Tasha standing before him dressed in hot pink lingerie. The communications were clear; there was no need for conversation. Not only had Tasha planned and set the scene, but she already had a good idea of how her partner would react.

The evening was a great success, and it led to some intimate conversation afterward. Sometimes the sex comes before the talk. It all depends on your plan. The Key is to make the decision to create the heat, and then make a plan that serves that purpose. If the unexpected happens, don't let that stop you from dropping back and huddling together to decide where to go from there. A different outcome than you planned doesn't have to be a game-stopper. Try a different approach; that's all.

CHAPTER 3

SECRET KEY #2

KNOW AND SHARE YOUR TURN-ONS

You can't share what you don't know. Before you can clearly communicate what makes you hot, you have to take a little self-inventory of your turn-ons. To give you some direction during your discovery process, we have listed some of the most common things that men and women say turns them on. Let's begin with ten things most men say are their hot buttons:

Ten Things Women Do That Make Men Hot

1. Men found it sexy when women take the initiative. If you're always the one to want sex, it can make you feel needy and undesirable. Knowing that your lady is looking at you with lust in her eyes is quite erotic. Everybody likes to feel wanted, and nothing sends that message better than a, well let's just put it bluntly, horny woman. If the decision to have sex is always initiated and led by the man, it's often difficult for the male to know if it is something his partner wanted to do or if she's just complying to get it over with so she can watch her favorite television program.

   The one who initiates sex also has a greater responsibility to make sure it's good. After all, you say to yourself; my partner is the one who wanted to do this—now, it's up to them to make me feel good. Having your partner hot for you takes the weight off your shoulders and lets you sit back and forget about all your cares and responsibilities. It sets your mind free and allows you to focus on all the pleasure your partner is giving you. Not that it is like this all the time, and that's the beauty. But, wow! Who wouldn't like to have those roles changed every once in a while?

2. Men loved their women to wear sexy lingerie or dress the part of the seductress. One gentleman said his partner would do her housework around him in nothing but a thong and stilettos. When I asked him if she ever got tired of walking around the house cleaning in high heels, he laughed. He eventually hired a housekeeper because her cleaning efforts never got any further than a few pushes with the vacuum and a deep bend in front of him with a dust cloth.

Sexy lingerie or skimpy underwear is nothing new as a turn on for men. Some like lingerie so see-through that it's only a hint of covering over the most important parts. Some men like for their partners to leave a little more to the imagination. Or, they like a tightly laced corset with thigh-high nylons. To make it a sure thing, you may want to look through some lingerie photos online or in a magazine together to see what fuels the fire.

3. Foreplay is just plain fun. Women are not alone in their love to practice tantalizing foreplay. When someone else controls the foreplay, the heat can build to such a crescendo that it threatens your ability to hang on and wait for your partner to reach your ready level. Foreplay can be a number of things, and it doesn't always have to end in intercourse. Some men find it blissfully torturous to have a woman that is proficient in blue-balling. The rise and fall of arousal can build the heat to such intensity that intercourse is almost anticlimactic.

4. Then there are the rather adventurous men who said they loved to watch their woman masturbate and climax as they were instructed on what to do to themselves. They liked seeing the confidence of a woman who wasn't afraid of her sexuality and who didn't act ashamed of her body. Many men also enjoyed the power they have over their partner when they bring her to orgasm.

5. Some men liked to hear the sound of excitement from their partners. They got turned on as their partner's breathing became labored, and then when moans escaped, their need heated up several degrees. Some liked to hear their names spoken or called out. Some wanted it loud and demanding. Others enjoyed just a hint of heat; a soft, horse released breath did the trick. Talking dirty is also an option, but for some partners that can be a definite turn-off. Make sure you define your turn-ons before putting them into play.

6. Some men enjoyed it when their partners squeezed their buttocks or their biceps in the heat of the moment, lifting themselves to the motion of their bodies. Without exception, men said they liked their partners to actively participate, to do a little grind during the foreplay. Some even wanted their partners to guide their hands to their "hot" spots.

7. Some got turned on by a woman's sense of humor, feeling secure in the knowledge that if he made a mistake, it wasn't going to be

earth shattering. It was a turn-on to know that he could let go of the stress and worry to focus on the fun. Isn't that what sex should be—playful and fun?

8. Many men liked their partners to be creative, unafraid to have fantasy sex, willing to have sex on the beach or in their friend's home as they visited for dinner. Anything that added that extra little bit of danger and excitement was enough to turn those embers into a fire.

9. Hands down, every man loves head. There is something empowering to men to see their partner go down on them and take their manhood in their mouth. One thing to agree upon before giving head is what you want to have happen at the point of climax. That way your man won't be distracted by wondering if he should pull out or not. Giving head is an excellent way to bring your partner to peak level, and then making them wait a bit and settling down until you build the next wave of pleasure. Get up for a minute, walk around nude, stand in front of the bed and let them

see your body's responses to his excitement. Then, start all over again. I'm getting hot just talking about it.

10. Most men wanted their partners to be up for anything, open to trying different ways to create hot sex. They wanted their partners to trust them enough to consider extreme fantasies and creative ways to light them up (7).

Okay, now that you know some of the things that men said turned them on, let's discuss what turns on women. Keep in mind; women are more complex creatures when it comes to their sexuality. A woman's turn-ons are often connected to emotional responses as well as their physical needs.

Ten Things Men Do That Make Women Hot

1. Women often preferred the lighter touches along their arms, down their backs, on their inner thighs, and brushed against their lips. What can be a turn-off is men who smash into their lips, open their

mouths so wide they could swallow a watermelon, and cram their tongues down their throats until they are ready to choke. Even if you're having rougher sex, it never hurts to pull back and lightly appreciate her skin and lips.

2. Most women loved to have their partners run their fingers through their hair. Of course, not when she's all ready to go out, but sitting on the couch during a make-out session or foreplay, scoop her hair back and even hold it a little tighter at the nape of her neck. It's a promise of gentle yet powerful sex. Very hot, guys!

3. Not only did women love the fresh smell of their partners, but they also enjoyed the act of showering together. It can be quite hot to feel each other's slick, soapy skin. A creative combination might be to wash your partner's hair for her while you're showering together. Now you're thinking! Spooning with your partner in the shower lets them feel the full pressure of your excitement as you run your fingers over her breasts, stomach, and down to her most private places.

4. Women found intelligence a turn-on. They liked their men to know about different things and be willing to talk about what they know. They wanted a man smart enough to challenge them and press them to be better. The mind is probably one of the most neglected sexual parts of one's body. When your partner can capture your thoughts, you can get lost in the process.

5. Women also enjoyed being surprised. Not just presents, either, although they're certainly welcomed once in a while. Surprises come in many different packages. Sometimes a surprise could be fixing the leaking sink that you promised to do two months ago, or making arrangements to have a meal catered in one night. If you want to make it a sexual surprise, linking it with food is always fun. The old whip-cream standby is good, then add a few strawberries and a few ice cubes from your drink, viola—you've got a hot surprise.

6. Women also loved partners who were patient with them. Don't get angry if they got home from work a little late. Avoid losing your temper with them when they take longer than you would like when it comes to putting on their makeup. Regarding foreplay, patience is a total turn-on. Wait for your partner's legs to shake and for her begging to begin before penetration. Believe me; that will sometimes take the patience of a saint—but the heat a patient partner creates is worth the wait.

7. Seductive texting was also a turn-on for women, especially when they'd had a particularly trying day. Instead of asking them what happened, tell your partner you have a way to take her mind off her problems and you plan on showing her when she gets home. Then, make the evening be about her. Give her a massage, from her shoulders, down her back, around to her inner thigh, and to her feet. Use a lubricant, and warm it up to warm her up.

8. Understanding a woman's personal needs will let her know that you know her inside and out. If she is grumpy, don't always think

it's something you did, just give her some space. Don't worry the situation or take the blame for something with which you are probably not involved. Don't get pouty and quiet; your partner deserves the chance to express her feelings even if she's grumpy or in a mood. Let her have those feelings, and welcome her back with open arms when she's ready to confide in you. If she doesn't feel like talking, call it good, and cuddle. With her distractions, this may not be a very good time for hot sex, but soft touches and cuddling can let her know you're sensitive to her needs.

9. Women like a well-dressed, freshly scented partner. Be careful about using cologne that's too heavy; you don't want to cover up the delicious smell of hot sex. Have you ever noticed that? Sex has such a warm glowing fragrance to it; you may just want to use soap as a scent and then let your manliness come through. Whenever you go out, your partner is wearing you like a designer accessory. So, make her proud!

10. Most women wanted to hear about their partner's feelings and beliefs. They wanted to know they were special enough for their man to share with them their deepest thoughts and secrets. Talking in bed after sex is an excellent time to do this. It increases the intimacy. Who knows, you could be headed for another fire (8).

You may not know yourself well enough or have enough confidence to voice your turn-ons to your partner. That's cool! The process of discovery will be eye-opening. You'll discover, and it will become quite obvious to your partner, the things that send you to the moon and back. If you can't tell your partner with words what you want, show him or her with sexy sounds and let your body speak for you at first. When you see how the Keys turn on the heat, you'll soon find the words to share with your partner all the things you want to have done to you and what you plan to do in return.

Try some of these Key things on yourself and with your partner to kick up the heat. Anticipate the amazing sex you'll have together, and share your imaginations and fantasies with your partner. Tell him or her what you plan on doing, and as you're exchanging likes and dislikes, a little bit of showing will go a long way to fan the sexual flames. All I've got to say is—enjoy the fire!

CHAPTER 4

SECRET KEY #3

MAINTAIN THE MYSTERY

Insert chapter five text here. Insert chapter five text here. Insert chapter Practicing this Key can be challenging, so let me explain what I mean by maintaining the mystery in your relationship. Can you remember how you felt about your partner when you began your relationship? You were both eager to learn about one another. It seemed like you just couldn't get enough. You weren't just hungry for their body, but you wanted to have it all—to consume and fold them into you until you knew one another's thoughts before they were spoken words.

Wanting to know everything about your partner isn't really what you desired, though. What most people seek is the "want." You want to still "want" to know more about your partner. Does that make sense?

When you quit wanting more, you quit altogether. It's the desire that drives the relationship—that creates the intimacy that reignites the fire of your relationship.

Mysterious doesn't mean manipulative. Don't play games to purposefully make your partner doubt your relationship or your devotion. That's unfair and cruel, and it will end up backfiring on you in the long run. Being a bit mysterious just means holding back a little for later, saving part of yourself so that your partner enjoys the discovery process. When he or she asks you something, instead of answering, let them know that you'll tell them later. Or, talk to them about how to find the answer to that one for themselves.

Be genuine and honest with your partner when you are creating or maintaining the mystery in your relationship. Those of you who have been in a relationship for a long time are probably thinking—it's a bit late for this Key, right? Wrong! For you, instead of holding information back and being mysterious, you have to create new mystic—but how? That's Key #3.

Give Cause to Question

When I say cause to question, I don't mean for you to give your partner cause to question your devotion or loyalty. Give him or her cause to wonder what you have up your sleeve—what is coming next. Be unpredictable. Do the unexpected. Keep your partner guessing, and make it fun and playful. For example, Clair curled up with a good book one cold winter evening. The fire was going, but there was a chill in the air, so she had her flannels on and a cozy cover-up as she laid beside her sweetie on the sofa. You wouldn't exactly call her pajamas sexy, but what she did with them started to light Patrick up.

She pulled the covers up to right below her neck as she read her book. At first, Patrick didn't look to see what she was reading. In fact, he paid little attention to Clair at all. He was busy streaming Facebook and checking his emails. So, she laid her book, print down, on the table so Patrick could see that it was an erotic book. Still acting like nothing was up as she adjusted the covers; then she picked the book back up and continued to read. Only, now that he saw the cover of the book, she had captured his interest. Next, Clair pulled off the bottoms to her pajamas and began playing beneath the covers, while still holding the book. The action beneath the blanket started getting more heated, and Patrick wanted in on the action. It was a fun evening, and it wasn't long before neither Clair nor Patrick needed the covers or the fire; they were making a fire together that made the one in the fireplace unnecessary. Clair never turned a page of that book, and Patrick never noticed because he was busy under the covers with Clair.

The reason I share this story with you is that Clair did the unpredictable, and it ended in great sex. She didn't sit down to have a big talk with Patrick; she just started building the fire all by herself and Patrick joined in. What she did was peak Patrick's curiosity, and then teased him into being attentive. There was no nagging or anger, just playful fun. Not only did Clair capture Patrick's attention, but because she has continued now and then to do the unpredictable, Patrick looks forward to what's coming next—besides him.

Another element of Clair's sofa surprise is that she kept herself hidden. What is hidden is often more enticing than what is offered in plain sight. If someone walks along a nude beach sporting a skimpy bathing suit while all the other beach people are stark naked, who do you thing gets the most attention? You guessed it, the one that left a little to the imagination.

Don't Always Be Readily Available

It may sound like you're game-playing, and perhaps in a way you are. However, it's a healthy game designed to keep the fire burning in your relationship. What I mean by not always being readily available is this. Don't wait by the phone, picking it up on the first ring, out of breath as if you ran to answer. Don't ask when your partner is going to call, just expect that he or she will. If they tell you they'll give you a call, let them know that you have plans and may not be home so they can leave a message and you'll call them back later. Now you've got them wondering where you are going, who you'll be with, and when you'll call them back. You've created some mystery.

Being needy with your partner is like pouring water on the fire. Rarely do others enjoy having to reassure someone all the time by reporting their whereabouts. Don't become an extension of your partner—get a life! Be active with friends of your own. Avoid making your partner responsible for planning your daily activities. In fact, he or she doesn't need to be included in everything you do.

Don't Talk Too Much

No matter if your relationship is new or you have years of familiarity with one another, avoid talking non-stop about every little insignificant detail of your day. Don't write on your Facebook about everything you did during the day. Although it's great to share things with your lover, does your partner need to know you just picked up a Starbuck's latte? Sometimes, it's fun to send a text to say—*"Guess where I am?"* Then don't respond when he or she returns the text. As predicted, as soon as your partner gets home, he or she will probably be asking about that text.

People who talk too much about themselves can completely shut down their partners with the same old boring chit-chat. Learn to be an attentive listener. Get your mind out of yourself and into your partner. When you talk, share things that matter to your partner—perhaps something new you discovered about his or her favorite activity, sport, or hobby. Let them know you are thinking of them.

Some Things Are Better Left to the Imagination

This is especially true if you've been together for quite some time and the fire in your relationship is only showing a few flumes of smoke— if that. What I mean by this is, when you're doing private things, to keep them private. For example, when you use the potty, shut the door. When you are coloring your hair, do it at a time when your partner is out with friends. When the "boys" are itchy, avoid spreading your legs open on the couch in front of the game and giving yourself a three-minute scratch down. Believe me, when I tell you, this is far from a fire builder. Some things are better done in private.

Most bathroom grooming should be done alone unless of course, you're using the shower as an enticement. Make the bathroom a place of sexy fun, not a place where your partner is exposed to all your daily duties. If your dog leaves the bathroom when you've entered, it's a clear sign that what routinely goes on in there needs to be private. Enough said!

Challenge Your Partner

A little healthy competition can raise the heat in a relationship. Competitive activites should be something that you enjoy together. If you have a sport that both of you participate in, make it competitive. If you don't do any activities together, you've got to challenge yourself to find one. It's important that you find activities that can be enjoyed together. It gives you something to talk about and a time of fun together. It also lets you show off your prowess and strength. If the sport is swimming, that could open up a whole new set of skills.

Challenging your lover doesn't always have to be in the form of sport. You can test them in a computer game, playing cards, or even just making a bet. Who knows, the payoff can be quite rewarding for both of you.

Let Your Partner Earn Your Compliments

Avoid fishing for compliments—it's just another way you show your insecurities. Women can be particularly guilty of this. They'll ask if they look too fat in this outfit, or become offended if their partner doesn't compliment their new hairdo or designer shoes. One lady has a unique way of knowing when her rather undemonstrative partner thinks she looks extra special. He has a dead giveaway sign that he's impressed. He raises his eyebrows when he sees her. That's all—raised eyebrows?

Yep, what this woman has learned is to recognize even the smallest signal from her partner. She knows she looks good, and she's never been one to like lavish compliments. Instead, she searches her partner's face for those telltale raised brows to celebrate her exceptional appearance. What's more, she's learned to return the favor. There have been times when they are across the room at a party, and she will give him that look, raise a dainty little brow, touch her finger to her parted lips, and build a long-distance fire that they both know won't be able to be enjoyed for a few hours. The anticipation is deliciously hot.

Encourage Silent Communication

These kinds of communications are only between the two of you, creating together the mystery that nobody else can share. These types of silent communications should be little tidbits of information to which only you and your partner are privy. For instance, you may want to whisper in your lover's ear as you go into a restaurant that you feel naked without wearing panties, or ask him to see if he thinks anyone could tell that you are not wearing a bra.

One gentleman told me of a time he was at his tennis club, and he found himself being turned on by watching his lover compete in the final round. After she had won the match, he gave her their silent signal, and together they celebrated her win in the club's darkened supply room. Everyone had left, or so they hoped, and it was just them, the linens, and that lovely musky smell of hot sex. The point is, they had a shared secret, a wonderfully mysterious way to communicate their needs that left out the rest of the world.

Create the Mystery

When you have been together for quite some time, it takes a bit more work to create mystery in your relationship. You have already shared so much information and know each other so well, that you can practically finish one another's sentences. So, you may think this Key is not going to be possible for you. Not so! It may be a little more challenging for you to create opportunities to be mysterious, but that element of surprise and the knack of being unpredictable will be your ticket to success.

Speaking of tickets, one lady shared this interesting story. She felt her partner needed a little space in their relationship. So, she bought tickets for him and a buddy to go to the football game. When she gave him the tickets, she also informed him that she'd be waiting for him when he returned with another surprise. Then she said, if the lights are out when you get home, don't sit down and snack in front of the television. Come on into the bedroom. I'll be waiting there for you with your surprise.

He was so excited thinking about what she had planned that there were times he found it impossible to focus on the game. Although his buddy wanted to stop for a drink after the game, her partner politely refused. He had better things to do.

Creating and maintaining the mystery in a relationship builds excitement and anticipation of a hot encounter. It takes planning and effort, but the results are well worth it. This, in fact, is one of the Keys that can be the most fun and playful. The fire that these sexual games put into your relationship is so memorable that just reminding your partner of them at another time will tease the senses.

I challenge you to be creative with this Key and make your sex unique and individual. Create private communications and develop an intimate language that is only understood by you and your partner.

CHAPTER 5
SECRET KEY #4

CHANGE IT UP

Although we've talked a great deal about different things you can do to build the heat, keep in mind anything you repeatedly do creates a routine. Between the games, the positions, the toys, and techniques, sometimes your partner just wants comfortable, nurturing, gentle love-making for a change. All of the Keys you use are designed to please and stimulate, but changing things up lets you excite your partner and have great sex irrespective of their attitude or mood.

To know when to play and when to put playfulness aside and just focus on body worship, you have to be able to read your partner. Being attentive and sensitive to your partner's feelings and emotions are paramount to using these Keys. Your flexibility and desire to please your partner must trump your desire to please yourself. If your partner needs to be nurtured and cuddled, then that should be your focus. If your partner needs to feel empowered, then do what's necessary to fulfill that need.

We've offered you a treasure chest of golden Keys to reignite the fire in your relationship, but being willing to change and use these Keys will determine how much heat you can create. To continue to build the fire, refuse to allow yourself to do one thing most of the time. Change things up, be creative, be unpredictable, be fun and playful, be tender, be rough—but most of all be knowledgeable about all the things you can do to keep the fire burning.

The idea of changing things up is not just a clever ploy; it's a scientific fact that people need change. Studies have shown that dopamine decreases over time with the same sexual partner. Does this mean you must find another partner? Not necessarily. Let's discuss how our dopamine levels come into play when we're feeling all the pleasures of incredible sex.

I don't mean to over-simplify, but I also don't want to reduce dopamine into a scientific discussion about neurons and transmitters, either. Dopamine is commonly called the pleasure chemical. It is that magical molecule that gladly supports all our most sinful habits and cravings, as it passes along pleasure signals to reward us when we have sex or feel lustful. Increases in dopamine keep us coming back for more. Sometimes you don't even have to have sex, just be reminded of it when smelling perfume or cologne associated with an exciting sexual encounter, and your dopamine levels begin to increase (9).

Changing it up can cause the sexual excitement that stimulates an increase in dopamine levels, making it possible to have hot sex without the need to change partners every few months. The more creative and imaginative you are when it comes to changing things up, the greater your chances will be to reignite the fire in your current relationship. Emotionally bonding with another partner takes time and energy, so why not build a sensual fire with the person to whom you are already attached?

Not only can you change things up by creating mystery and employing new devices that stimulate your imagination as well as your body, but you can change where and when you have sex as well. Once you have experimented in every room in your home, take it outside. Expand your sex to include public places where the chances of you getting caught increase your excitement. Talk about sex and get your partner aroused at a time when there is no possible way to satisfy your need for hours, and then watch the fire build. Tory and Malcolm know the value of applying this Key to their sex life.

Malcolm teased Tory late one afternoon before going to their in-laws for dinner. They showered together, getting one another quite lathered up, and then Malcolm remembered something he had to do before leaving. In a rush, with many apologies, he hoped out of the shower, leaving Tory in a state of unsatisfied heat. All the way to his in-laws, Malcolm kept saying that he was sorry and promised to make it up to her later. This only served as a reminder of what she had missed.

The whole evening, Malcolm would glance at Tory, with a promise of pleasure when they got home, and all the while Tory and Malcolm's dopamine levels were skyrocketing. Every once in a while, Malcolm would slide his hand up Tory's leg beneath the table to keep her body engaged as well as her mind. Dinner ended early that evening, and they rushed back home for a desert of a different kind.

Changing it up almost always involves some additional tools of the trade, you just need to be sure you are both in agreement with whatever activities sound interesting. If you lack imagination and creativity, watch the movie *"Fifty Shades of Grey,"* and pick up some helpful information. Not that you'll want to go to that extreme, but experimenting is allowed. While you're at it, watch the movie with your partner. It will give you a chance to build and fire and discuss your sexual likes and limits.

Tools and Toys

To help you out, we have included some interesting tools and toys to enhance your sex life. The beauty of these devices is that you can shop for them discreetly online. If you have done so, you'll be quite entertained by their variety and scope. You'll find toys that vibrate, gyrate, and pulsate. You'll find devices in all colors and textures, with ones designed to fit inside, outside, and even on your fingers. For those of you who plan on water sports, you'll be happy to know that many are toys are waterproof. If your changeup includes postponing sex and building the fire, you'll find devices that can be worn in the underwear or tucked securely inside the body that can be controlled remotely. These types of toys can create a whole other kind of mystery and secret signal, right?

Sexually stimulating toys are not just to pleasure women, but many are specially designed just for men. What used to be intimidating for men is now not only acceptable but eagerly anticipated. An online survey was done in 2014 of 5,000 men. The study was conducted to discover how men felt about the use of sex toys. They found that 51 percent of men owned sex toys, 60 percent said they had used them on their partners, and it was extremely enjoyable.

Included in these toys for men are vibrating cock rings, to contain the heated variety if that peaks your interest. There are butt plugs, and sleeve or pocket vaginas that can be filled with a wide range of excitable ingredients. If anything, just shopping for the toys can be an awesome experience for you and your partner. Shop together and double your fun. It's a great way to introduce the new possibilities, to bring up the fact that you want to increase the heat in your sex life. Just tell your partner you want to do some online shopping together for some special surprises.

For you who enjoy living on the edge, there are the extreme toys. These are used in couples' bondage games which combine pleasure with a little sting. They include floggers, blindfolds, ropes, handcuffs, and chains. These types of toys are usually for the more seasoned sexual appetites, but having a knowledge of such activities is a good thing just in case you decide to take a giant step outside your comfort zone.

It's a good thing most people are past the idea that sex toys are weird, and boy are we past it! Adult toys in North America alone is a $500,000 a year industry, worldwide it has exploded to a multi-billion-dollar business (10). The choices are endless, and they also include lubricants, which can be purchased as all natural, organic, and water soluble products. There are lubricants that provide various sensations, like tingling, warmth, and icy cool, so you can experiment and determine which ones tickle your fancy. They come in almost any flavor under the sun or have no taste at all. Some are smooth textured, and some are granulated. So many choices—so little time.

Pricing for your sex toys is about as varied as the products, beginning as low as $5 on up to $200 plus. My point is, and I hope this important Key has demonstrated that there are so many things you can incorporate into your sex life to reignite the fire in your relationship. Some techniques or toys you may not like, but you won't know how to change it up without doing some investigating. You will know your partner's likes and dislikes better if you explore your options together, and now you can do so in the privacy of your home.

CHAPTER 6

SECRET KEY #5

CONNECTING ON ALL SEXUAL CYLINDERS

Connecting with your partner on all levels takes your experience a whole level up. No-emotion sex is good, but when you connect physically and emotionally, it's unbelievable. The more you can connect with your partner, the more you'll want to. All the games, toys, movies, lingerie, or erotica cannot give you that "as one" connection if it doesn't come with deep emotional commitment to your partner. That's what is called connecting on all sexual cylinders.

When the heat is high and so is your emotional connection, sex becomes love-making. When your fire is burning strong, and you're implementing all the Keys you've learned, your love-making can reach euphoric heights.

It takes all the Keys. You have to make a conscious decision to build the heat into your relationship. Then, discover and share your turn-ons with your partner. Be unpredictable, do the unexpected to maintain some mystery in your relationship. Get creative and be willing to change it up so that the fire doesn't die. Lastly, apply all the Keys to keep the fire going, each partner eager to experience the next sexual encounter.

This is your opportunity to transform yourself into a sexual beast. At work you may be the best nurse or lawyer, but once you get home, you can change into a pornstar. Okay, it doesn't have to be that extreme, but you will discover some additional perks when you can heat up your relationship. Great sex can change other aspects of your life as well.

Hot Sex Can Change Your Professional Prowess

When you are more confident with your sexual self, it changes your level of confidence and your ability to communicate. Let's face it, the more confident you become, the more likely you are to be valued at work. When you are perceived as a valued worker, the monetary rewards soon follow. Also, your ability to communicate is greatly enhanced with a "hotter" sex life. Why? To have a great sex life, you have to be an excellent communicator—with your body language as well as your words.

Today's workers, whether white or blue collar, deal with a tremendous amount of stress. If that pressure is allowed to build, it can turn you into a discontent complainer. Your energy level goes down, and you find yourself depressed and unhealthy. Before you realize it, you're taking more sick days or personal time, and still you feel tired. Those who allow themselves to be lackluster sexual partner soon become unenthusiastic business partners.

Hot sex also makes the participants able to concentrate and focus more at work. Once you've learned the Five Keys to reigniting your relationship, you have to get creative and be determined to put them into practice. Your focus and concentrated effort brings you great rewards, and so your brain begins to conceive of other ways to focus and concentrate. It's only natural that you take these skills to the workplace.

Also, practicing the Five Keys taps into your creative side. Even those that haven't previously considered themselves to be imaginative will be much improved after implementing the Five Keys into their relationships. That same creative effort will also spread into your career efforts, giving you the willingness to try different problem-solving strategies or office management techniques. By building the fire in your relationship, you can also create greater opportunities for success in other areas of your life.

Hot Sex Makes You More Attractive

Have you ever heard people say, *"Oh, you must have got some last night?"* Even if you didn't, why would people say that? It's because most people recognize the difference in one's appearance when they have recently had hot sex. Their skin glows. They walk taller. Their smile is wider. They're more patient. They're more accepting of new ideas. It's a commonly accepted fact that people who regularly have great sex are just more fun to be around. More people are attracted to individuals who ooze sexual energy, and you can't help but do so when you're still experiencing the aftermath of an intense sexual encounter.

I've heard it said that sexier people are more active and that increased activity helps you to be less stressed and more youthful. When you are enjoying a raging fire in your relationship, you'll want to look and feel your best outside the bedroom. Your body image will improve, and you will have a little spring in your step (11).

You'll Identify with Your Newly Discovered Sexuality

Many people who have accepted a life of boring sex or no sex at all, have learned to compartmentalize their lives. They often will share with their closest confidant that their relationship is great—all but the sex, that is. What they have done is create a separate box in which to store their unsatisfactory sex. Once tucked away, it doesn't have to cause them discomfort or embarrassment anymore. These people have become masters at disassociating their sex lives from all the other elements that make them unique.

Just as those having great sex become better all-around individuals, people who suffer the pangs of separating their souls from their sex lives begin to see the negative impact that separation can cause in their lives. Our sexual prowess has a direct correlation with our self-perception and how others see us as well. Like it or not, we are often defined by our sexuality.

If you want to experience life to its fullest, you have to do it all— including sex. It isn't all about sex, but sex is an important part of all our lives. If sex is so important to our well-being, then why settle for just "so-so" sex? Why not crank up the heat, ignite the flame of desire you once had and bring sex back to life? Nobody will appreciate it more than your partner— except maybe you.

You now have a sexual toolbox, filled with all the elements of the Five Keys. If these Five Keys are to be beneficial, you have an important choice to make. Do you finish the book and do nothing, wishing off and on you had the nerve to apply the Keys to your sex life? Or, do you get started immediately on ways to build a fire in your relationship? It's imperative to know that by saying yes to change, it will require something from you. You now have a responsibility to do the work, to keep the fire burning, to increase the heat, and to share more of yourself with your partner.

All strong people have vulnerabilities; all have weaknesses that can either be hidden or used to bring about great changes in their lives. Your sexuality carries with it great power, opportunities, and incredible rewards if you say yes to putting the Five Keys to work for you and your partner. By applying these Keys, you and your partner's lives will be enriched and energized. It won't take long, either. Just a lot of practice, but who's going to complain about having more fiery sex?

It's never too late to practice the Five Keys. If you think your relationship is too cold to try, what have you got to lose? If you or your partner is about to walk anyway, you've got nothing to lose, right? If you move on to greener pastures, you can pack up your Keys and take them with you. If you have no partner to practice them with, that's okay. You can practice alone and get to know your turn-ons that much better. If you are to have a start-over, you will know better this time around.

However, if there are still some embers burning in this relationship, try rekindling them. Even if you have some other challenges, all relationships have challenges. Guess what? Many of those challenges are caused by boring sex or no sex at all. The decision you make right now can be life altering, no kidding! Don't believe me? Give it a try—see for yourself. All it takes is a decision to apply the Five Keys and bring on the heat, in this relationship or another.

Have you decided? Good! Now turn off the television, slip into something more revealing, put down this book, and let it burn, baby.

PART V

CHAPTER 1

WHAT ARE THESE SECRET KEYS TO A RELATIONSHIP BREAKTHROUGH?

Have you ever wondered why so many people fail in their relationship with men, whether as friends or more than that? Wondered why so many couples break up, even though it seemed like they would be together forever? Do you have a hard time connecting with men enough to take your relationship to the highest level possible? Many people do, and that is because they do not know about these secret keys for a breakthrough.

It is essential to know what men want and need, otherwise, you will not be able to know him as well as you wish you could, and the distance will make it hard to connect. A connection is important when in a relationship, as it is what determines the amount of passion you have years down the road. A weak connection makes for weak passion and limited intimacy once the honeymoon phase is over.

If you do not have passion and intimacy in a marriage, this can be a major problem, as they are what keep the love alive, and the marriage interesting. Without any interest in your marriage, it can cause many problems, including divorce, and infidelity.

So to avoid these issues you must learn about the secret keys, for without them you will be destined to have an average relationship, rather than a superb relationship. Which an average one can last forever, but a superb relationship will most definitely last forever.

Only about twenty percent of people know about these keys to a man's heart. They are the couples that you see that are eighty years old and still acting like young lovers. They are the couples that everyone aspires to be. These people are the happiest couples alive because they learned the secret keys to marriage, and to unlock their man's heart.

Why it is Pertinent to Know these Keys

These keys are the basis of obtaining a strong and intimate relationship. Almost everyone's goal in life is to get married, and have that marriage last forever. They want to be the couple that everyone looks up to, and that everyone comes to for advice.

That is where these keys come in. They are designed to help you achieve that level of a relationship in your life. These are from a man's perspective, to help you understand more what they really want. Not what women say they want.

A man's heart is unique. It is unlike a woman's heart in many ways, and should be treated as such. You should want to know exactly how to open his heart to show you exactly how he wants to be loved.

Men are also stubborn at times. You may have already won his heart, but he has put up walls to try to prevent himself from falling. You have to break through these walls as well, which if you use these keys, should be easier than just whacking away at it with charm. Read on to find these keys.

Chapter 2:

Secret Key #1

Desire

Men do not say this aloud, which is why this key is such a big secret, but men love romance. They want their partners to put in a little romantic effort as well. This key is important, as without it, a man cannot be sure if you are really down for him or not. If he doesn't feel like you desire him, he will not completely open up to you. Very few couples realize how important this is, and that is why often times, you see relationships fizzle out so fast. Follow this key to strengthen your bond with the male species.

Romance

Describe your most romantic fantasy. Is it elaborate? Or simple? Either way, you most likely still have one. So does he. Men are romantic creatures by nature, but they also like to be romanced. Take him out to dinner, and pick up the check. Take him out to the movies, and pay for him. Return the favor he probably often shows you quite frequently.

It doesn't even have to be that expensive either. When he has a long day at work, surprise him with his favorite dinner served by candlelight. In his day off, pack a picnic lunch, and drive to his favorite spot and enjoy a picnic. It doesn't have to always be fancy, you just need to put in as much effort into showing him you want him, as he does for you.

It is about feeling wanted, and loved. If you aren't putting in an effort to show him how much you care, how is he going to know that you are going to be there in the long run? He will feel like you are only there for what he can do for you, not what you can do together, and he will begin to feel used. Value a man. Don't expect to get treated like royalty if you are only going to treat him like a peasant.

To understand more about being romantic for a guy, this scenario will help you to understand more, that it isn't always about the big things, sometimes even the smallest gesture means the world to a guy.

Scenario

James looked over at his girlfriend, and wondered if she truly loved him. She said it all the time, but how did he know for sure? Was she just fronting to get his money or was she truly his ride or die chick? How could he be sure that she really loved him?

"Babe?" He called over to MaryBeth

"Yes, baby?" She replied

"Answer three questions for me. What is my favorite color? What was my favorite memory as a child? What is my favorite food?" James needed to know if she loved him as much as he loved her. He knew that her favorite color was purple, because it reminded her of the twilight hours when everything is quiet and still. He knew that her favorite childhood memory was when her dad took some free bikes and pieced them together to make her very first bike because they were too poor to buy a new one. He knew that her favorite food was Italian, and that it only became so when she met him, because he was Italian, and showed her how real cuisine was created, rather than restaurants that order frozen food and heat it up in a microwave. He wanted to see if she knew the answers to those questions.

"You don't have a favorite color, per say. You are color blind. You say that your favorite color would be emerald green because that is the color I told you my eyes were. Your favorite childhood memory was when you and your brother climbed the big oak tree in your backyard together, and talked about life and what your plans were for your futures. You said that was the first time you two had really ever bonded, and that was when you realized you wanted to be a real estate investor. You were nine. Your favorite food is Chinese, because it reminds you of when your mother used to take you to a Chinese restaurant every Friday for mother-son bonding time. The last time you did that with her was two days before she died. You used to dislike Chinese food, but went because she loved it, but after she died, the memories made you love it." She answered. "Now tell me. What is this about?"

"I was wondering if you loved me. No girl has ever paid enough attention to me, and focused mainly on my wallet. You answered every question perfectly. The first one to ever do so. I love you so much."

"How could you doubt I love you, James? I may not have a lot of money, but I try to show you every day that I love you. You should think about that, rather than focusing on little questions that anyone who pays attention to you could answer." MaryBeth replied, slightly offended that he felt she didn't love him.

As she walked out of the room, James sat and thought about what she said. He thought back over the course of their relationship, and thought about all the things she did for him regularly.

She cooks me dinner on a regular basis. When I have had a hard day, she rubs my back. Even though she is on her feet for over eight hours a day, and mine is just stress of a tenant not wanting to pay rent. She shows up on my longer days with my favorite meal, and we eat it together before we have to go back to work. For no reason at all, she told me to get in the car, and we drove to our favorite spot with some fast food, and ate while watching the trains pull into the station.

She always tells me she loves me before she goes to bed, even if she is angry with me. She never fails to ask me how my day was, and truly listen to the answer. Even though sometimes I tune her out when she talks about hers. I don't know what her favorite song is, or when her first heartbreak happened, but she sure as hell know mine. What have I done for her? I know the answer to three questions that anyone with half a brain could answer, and I buy her stuff. I take her out to fancy dinners, and spend money on her but that is about it, and yet she never questions my love for her. I want to marry this woman. She is my everything. She has a piece of me that no one else ever will. She truly has my heart.

James walked back into the bedroom, where he found MaryBeth crying. He sat beside her, and began to rub her back.

"I'm sorry. I am so sorry I ever doubted your love for me. I know I could say that every other girlfriend has only wanted my money, and it broke me, but in truth; I am just an ass. I love you, MaryBeth. I want to marry you someday. Not today, we still have a lot of things to work through, but if you forgive me, I promise that one day you will have an engagement ring on your finger." James said, pulling out a little ring and sliding it on her ring finger. "Do you accept my promise?"

"Yes. I forgive you as well." MaryBeth said, beaming with happiness while her eyes were still brimming with tears.

Discussion

James didn't realize until it was brought to his attention, all the little things that MaryBeth does for him to show her love. Sometimes you do have to give him a little wake up call to show him that you do play the romance card on a regular basis. Maybe do a big gesture here and there to really show him you care. But sometimes it just takes you telling him to think that gets his brain in gear. Be romantic, and even if he doesn't realize it at first, he will start to see all the little things you do for him, even when he doesn't notice you doing them.

Desire

You have to ignite a white-hot passion in him that makes him want to take you right here and right now almost any where you go. This desire is what fuels the passion in your relationship. If there is no passion, things get stale, and that is when people drift apart the most. If the bedroom isn't rocking, you better get packing, because you need a good sex life, and desire filled relationship to last for a long time.

How do you ignite this desire in him? It is simple. You have to desire him as well. Men are easily enticed, if you are willing to tap into your animalistic nature. You have to want to make him desire you, so that means you will have to be pro-active in your sexuality, and prove your prowess in the bedroom, along with outside the bedroom.

How is this done exactly? Ditch the missionary position. This is the bane of all sexual existence. There are so many more positions out there, where you don't have to lie there like a lifeless doll and take what he is giving you. (Ditch standard doggy style for gay couples. This is the missionary in the gay world.) Look up new positions and try them for yourselves. Try different styles. There are some that can spice up the bedroom if you are both willing to try it.

- BDSM: This is a type of sexual style that requires one partner to be dominant, and one partner to be submissive. Start out slow. Don't go "Fifty Shades of Grey" level the first day. Ease into it. Find out the limitations your bodies can handle, how tight you like the collars and ties, what you absolutely do not like, and so on and so forth. Knowing what you like is important, as if you don't like it, the experience will not be fun. Both of you have to be vocal if you want to know what each other likes and don't like. Also, come up with a safe word to use, so in the heat of the moment, you don't hurt yourselves.

- Roleplay: This is one for when you want to experience what it is like to have sex with someone different, yet still wanting that sex to be with your partner. You get little costumes, and you dress up as someone else. While dressed up as another person, you literally become that person. You are not yourself, you are a whole other person. This could mean you have your guy become the cable guy, or you become his secretary. There are many other people you can take on the role of, such as famous people, or make up your own personas. If you do not feel comfortable with role play, but are still intrigued by it, try it on a small scale. Have him be a fake person you make up, and vice versa. This will get you more comfortable with the idea, so you can more enjoy it.

- Making a Home Video: This can be a very good bonding experience in the bedroom, as you can watch back the video you make, and see how much you were enjoying the sex. Once you both realize how good things are in the bedroom, you will never want to leave. Relax and enjoy it, though. Don't try to put on a show just because you are being filmed. You aren't a porn star, and neither is he. Just enjoy it. You can also see what positions work for you, and what doesn't when you play the video back. These videos should never be put on the internet, or used for any other reason than your viewing pleasure. If handled correctly, they can make for great material to get you in the mood as well.

- Watch Porn Together: This can give you an idea on positions to try, and also get you in the mood to do the deed. Find a video that you both like, and settle in. You can also try a bit of self stimulation while watching the video, but be careful not to distract yourself, or your partner from the video itself. The whole point is to learn new positions and bond. Remember though, porn is an act. Do not expect to have super explosive orgasms the first time you try a position. You most likely will have to practice a few times for it to even feel good.

There are many ways to spark up some interest in the bedroom, but how do you make him want to do these things? How do you spark the carnal desire in him? How do you show him you want him so bad it makes your stomach do flips? There are a few ways that are fool proof.

- Send Him Little Notes: You can leave sticky notes all over the house for him, in his car, in his lunchbox if he has one. You can also text him all the things you would like to do to him. Tell him that you aren't wearing any underwear or something like that. Give him something to want later that night.

- Tease Him: Kiss him seductively in the hall way and then keep moving along. Rub your rear against his junk, and then walk away. Play footsie with him when you eat dinner. Make him desire you, turn him on, but then leave him hanging. At the end of the night he will want you so bad, he will do anything to have you.

- Be Playful: Sometimes the biggest turn on is when you act like a kid. Being free-spirited can be the biggest turn on for guys, because they like knowing you are happy and having fun. Tickle him, and then make him chase you to the bedroom and tackle you on the bed. Play wrestle a little bit, and watch the playing turn into sex real fast. Sometimes the best foreplay, is to simply play.

You have to create a white-hot desire in the pit of his stomach, one that makes him crave you when you are away, and not want to leave your side when you are near. You have to make him think about you constantly, to the point where he doesn't even want you to go to the restroom because that means being away from you for too long.

This desire will unlock the part of his heart that makes him want to commit. He won't want to leave, because he is too devoted to you, and he loves you way too much to walk away from everything you have together. You have to keep this desire alive, and strong, to keep the relationship strong and healthy.

Here is a scenario that should help you get a mental picture of what that desire looks like. Caution. This one is mildly graphic, but if you are an adult reading this, as the disclaimer warns, you have probably read much worse.

Scenario

He wanted her. He wanted her more than he has ever wanted anyone. The way she teased him drove him insane. It was like she took pleasure in keeping him aroused to the point of pain. She would pay for it, when she finally let him have her. These thoughts swirled around Mason's brain, and left him winded. He thought back to when they first met.

Lacy wasn't like a lot of girls. That is what attracted Mason to her. He was tired of girls throwing themselves at him. He was tired of girls who had nothing more to offer than a loose vagina, and some amateur head. These women bored Mason, so he never kept them around much longer than a night. Lacy, however, showed very little interest in Mason when they first met. She looked him up and down, offered her hand in a professional manner, and said it was nice to meet him. Like she was at a job interview. She didn't blush, or swoon, or make any indication that she found Mason attractive. He had to have her. She was exactly what he wanted. A challenging woman.

He became more and more infatuated with her as the night drew on, and he listened to her talk, and engaged in conversation with her. She was Harvard educated, and it showed. She wasn't haughty or anything, really she was very humble, but when she spoke her words were eloquent and well thought out. She didn't use 'like' in between every word, as most girls tend to do. Instead, every word out of her mouth was carefully planted like she was speaking a puzzle.

She turned him on. Plain, and simple. He had to have a date with her.

"Excuse me, Lacy? I am enamored by your eloquence, and would love to talk to you more, one-on-one. Would you care to have a cup of coffee with me after this party is over?" Mason asked

"Why don't we leave right now? I feel I am boring everyone else." Lacy said

"I highly doubt you are boring anyone, but if you wish, I would love to go at once."

They left the club, and walked down the street to a little coffee shop that was open twenty four hours a day. This was one of Mason's spots to think, and he wanted Lacy to experience it as well. When they walked in, he could tell that she was star-struck with the place. It wasn't well known, but it was cozy. He offered to buy her coffee, but she refused, stating that she was glad to have an excuse to leave the club.

"I hope you don't think that I am like other girls, Mason." Lacy said as soon as the found a cozy nook to sit down.

"I beg you are pardon?" Mason nearly choked on his latte

"I don't put out on the first date. You have to win my heart. You can't just bring me to a quaint little coffee shop, and expect me to sleep with you tonight." Lacy was blunt with what she spoke, there was no beating around the bush.

"Of course I don't think you are like other girls. In fact, I have never brought a woman here before."

As if on cue, the shop owner came out then to greet Mason.

"Mason, my old friend. Are you enjoying your evening? Oh! You have a lady with you! Forgive me for interrupting, I have never seen this before. Enjoy yourselves." The shop owner ducked back into his office with a bright red face.

"Well I guess I don't need to ask you to prove that you have never brought a woman here."

They sat and talked the night away. In the wee hours of the morning, Mason drove Lacy home, as her friends had already left the club.

"Lacy, can I see you again?" Mason asked, as she stepped out of the car.

"I would like that very much."

Three months later, Lacy practically lived with him. They often slept in the same bed. And he still had not been able to make love to her. That is what he wanted. He didn't want to just have sex with her, he wanted to make love to her.

"What is on your mind, Mace?" Lacy asked, sitting on his lap.

"I want you, Lacy. More than I have ever wanted anyone. I love you. I truly love you. I want to make passionate love to you, in a way no man ever has. I want to give you the world, if you will let me. You are the one I want. Forever."

"Mason, that is what I have been wanting to hear since we met. Tonight you will finally get what you want. Me."

That night was the most mind blowing night of Mason's life. Lacy felt perfect for him. They didn't leave the bedroom for hours. Everything was perfect.

Flash forward two years later, and Lacy still teased him. He still wanted her as much as he did from day one. He couldn't imagine life with any other woman, as she was the only one who lit such a desire in him.

Discussion

Lacy made Mason desire her, by not always being readily available. She let him know she was into him, but she did not give up everything from the beginning, and even after she gave it all up, she still kept that playfulness up in the relationship, making him want her bad enough to always desire her.

This is what you have to do in a relationship. You have to keep your partner interested in you. Don't think that just because you have been together for a long time, that means you have to act like an old couple. Be playful. Show each other how much you care.

Chapter 3:

Secret Key #2

Make Him Feel Safe

Men will never admit that they need to feel safe in a relationship. This key is a secret, because society makes men feel that they have to be macho all the time. This is the furthest from the truth, and you should not believe this, as everyone needs to feel safe. Not just physically, but emotionally.

Couples that know this often have less fights, and less time spent angry at each other. Fights and arguments do not stem from someone doing something that you don't agree with, they stem from being afraid that they are going to leave you. You get angry because you don't feel safe, and you are scared you are going to be left alone, so you throw up a wall. Men do the same thing as everyone else. Only they will never admit that is why they have a wall up.

You have to make him want to take all of his walls down and be open with you. Make him feel like you want to know everything about him. Not just where he grew up, what his favorite color is, and what music does he like. Ask him if he ever sucked his thumb, did he have a teddy bear or a blankie? What was his favorite television show growing up? Has he ever been in trouble? What are his aspirations, and fears? Ask him about his nightmares. Do not be satisfied with one word answers. Give him information about you every time he divulges something about himself.

Emotional Safety

You have to be his safety net as he is free-falling into love with you, just as he has to be yours. You have to catch each other, and you can't fall if you don't trust the other person with your heart. Be open always. You can't expect him to open up to you when you won't open up to him. It is a give and take relationship, when you want to unlock the part of his heart he holds dearest to him.

To make him feel emotionally safe, you have to let him know that you won't let him down. This often means listening to him talk about things you aren't necessarily interested in.

A man has to be able to cry around you to feel truly and completely safe in a relationship. Sometimes you have to assure him that it is okay to cry. Hold him when you see him having a weak moment, and let him know that sometimes even the strongest mountain breaks down. If he can't cry around you, he won't be truly open to you. Men are at their most vulnerable moments in life when they break down in front of someone, because they are bred to believe that crying means you are weak. So if a man finally cries in front of you, you have won his heart.

Here is a scenario of how to know if you make him feel emotionally safe.

Scenario

Josh loved his boyfriend very much, but he felt as if Alex was still closed off. Josh was definitely the more feminine of the two, so he was very open with Alex. Alex however, often changed the subject when it came to his past. Josh knew that Alex loved him, he just wasn't ready to completely open up. Josh was understanding, and never pushed, but still let his love know that he was there for him.

One day, Alex came home in a horrible mood. Josh didn't know what was wrong, but he ran up and hugged Alex anyway.

"Oh, baby, I can just tell you had a horrible day. Would you like to talk about it?" Josh asked.

"Actually I would like that very much, babe." Alex said with a tight throat.

"Come sit down darling, let me make you your favorite tea while you compose your thoughts."

Josh hurried off to the kitchen, while Alex sat down on the couch, looking lost and forlorn. Josh's hear broke just looking at how sad his love looked. After the tea finished brewing, Josh hurried back into the living room, and handed Alex his tea, made just the way he liked it.

"What happened love?" Josh asked gently.

"I guess there is no sense in beating around the bush. My brother is dead. He was shot in the head last night in a drug deal gone wrong." Alex said

"I am so sorry love. I didn't know you had a brother, but I am heartbroken for you nonetheless." Josh said, wrapping his arms around Alex.

"I didn't talk about him much because I was ashamed of him. He was a drug addict. He was always asking when he could meet you, and I always made excuses. I feel horrible now, because he was the only one who supported me when I came out as gay. My parents kicked me out, and he gave me a place to stay. He was the only family I had, and I judged him for something he had about as much control over as I do being gay." Alex broke down in tears.

Josh sat there and held Alex, his heart breaking for him, as it also beamed with love, because Alex was finally opening up to him. He was sad that Alex's only true family was dead, but happy that Alex trusted him enough to tell him everything. His heart swelled with love for the man in his arms crying his eyes out.

Discussion

Alex was very closed off when it came to talking about his past, because it hurt to much to talk about, and he didn't want to cry in front of Josh, and Josh felt distanced from Alex due to his wall he threw up. Once Alex finally started talking about himself, Josh knew that Alex truly loved him, and that he trusted him finally. This gave Josh a happy feeling, even in the midst of a sad time, which allowed him to truly comfort Alex in his moment of need.

Why Do You Need This Key Again?

This key is essential in opening up an intense bond between you and your partner. When you feel comfortable enough to be completely open with each other, you learn more about the other than you could ever imagine. This is important, because to truly love someone, you have to truly know them. Once you truly know everything about someone, loving them becomes a whole lot easier.

Chapter 4:

Secret Key #3

Respect and Compassion

What is the one thing that anyone wants more than anything in the world? That is right, respect. Respect is rated the number one thing that a person wants in life. It is even more of a priority than love, because you can't have love if you don't have respect.

Respect is what makes the world go round. Think Aretha Franklin. R-E-S-P-E-C-T. This song is about how just a little respect can make a world of difference. You have to respect your partner not only as your partner, but as a human being as well. You can't expect them to be perfect, and you have to respect that sometimes they have to make mistakes.

This is where compassion comes in. When your partner makes a mistake, it is always important to show them compassion and understanding. This way they know that you care enough to help them make it through the mistakes they have made.

Why is this a Secret Key?

Most people do not know that men need more respect and compassion in the relationship. Men are often more insecure then women, they are just better at hiding it. Respect and compassion assure him that you love him and care about him, and that he is good enough for you. If he feels that he is worthy of you, he will become the most devoted person you have ever met. This key unlocks the section in his heart tied to fidelity. If he feels worthy of you, he will do anything to stay there. If he does not feel worthy of you, he will look for someone who makes him feel worthy.

EGO

This all boils down to ego. A man's ego is a powerful thing. Sometimes, if not treated properly, he can become borderline narcissistic. If he feels that he is not getting the respect he deserves, he will look to get it in any way he can. This is where a lot of severe relationship problems stem from. Emotional abuse, physical abuse, infidelity. This is all a problem created when a man is beaten down. Not necessarily by you, but by the world. This is what causes people to split up, and can ruin what seemed to be a perfect relationship.

Men aren't always aware of their ego issues, so they can't tell you what they need. That is not to excuse a man who becomes abusive or a cheater, or even to say that a man is helpless. They know right from wrong, they just don't realize what is causing them to do wrong. If he is abusive or a cheater, then you should leave. No questions asked. Leave. However, if he is just being angry for no reason, maybe you aren't showing each other enough respect and compassion.

How to Show Him Respect

- Be there for him: If he has a gig, or something important, go with him. Even if you aren't interested. Being there for him, and respecting him enough to support him shows him how much you care. If he needs you to listen to him, do so. Let him rant on about something you don't care about, but pay attention. Just because you don't care doesn't give you a free pass to ignore him or tune him out.

- Respect His Privacy: Trust is a big thing in a relationship. Both parties need their privacy on some things, and breaking that privacy is saying that you don't trust your partner enough to give him space. A big thing that a lot of women do is go through his phone. If you can't trust him enough to leave his phone alone, you probably shouldn't be in a relationship. You also shouldn't snoop through his drawers or his personal things. Let him have his privacy, just as you want yours.

- Respect His Personal Space: You don't have to be together every free moment you both have. Sometimes, spending time apart when you have free time is a good thing. You can do your own thing, and don't have to worry about if the other person is having fun. Men need this personal space to unwind after a hard day. Women do as well, but we are focusing on men here. If he doesn't text you back immediately, he is probably in the shower or taking a nice hot bubble bath. It does NOT mean he is cheating on you. Let him have his space without worrying about him stepping out on you. If you trust and respect him, he most likely will not want to do anything to break that trust. But if you don't trust him, he might just give you a reason not to.

- Respect the Fact that He is Human: Men are not robots, and they are not slaves. He has needs, and he needs them tended to at times as well. You cannot expect him to wait on you hand and foot, yet not turn around to do the same for him. Also he will mess up.

Don't hang it over his head for the rest of his life. Get through it, and then get over it.

Those are some ways that you can show that you respect him. Men are easy to please, and as they do not have the hormone fluxes that women do, it is more straightforward, but you still have to dig a little to find out his needs. He will give you what you need, if you respect him enough to let him.

Compassion

Compassion is important for when he is having a hard day or makes a mistake. You have to be willing to be compassionate towards someone to ever make a relationship work. Compassion is the difference between healing his heart and breaking it. If you are compassionate, he will trust you with things he doesn't trust anyone else with.

How to Be Compassionate

- Take Care of Him: If he is having a bad day, cook for him. Clean for him. Rub his back and cuddle him. I know this new-age mentality is that women are not a man's slave and that he can do for himself. That may be true, but sometimes you have to take care of him. In return, he will take care of you.

- Be Understanding: Men are human, and they will mess up. Don't overreact if he buys they wrong type of toilet paper, or the wrong grade of milk. They don't always get everything right. You have probably messed up sometimes as well. Did he freak out over the little things? Relax. If he isn't out killing people, or cheating on you, then discuss it calmly on why you prefer things a different way, and then make like Elsa and 'Let it Go'.

- Don't Ridicule Him: If he is not as advanced as you in some areas, do not make him feel bad for it. If you can read the best, and he can do math the best, combine your strengths. Don't make him feel like less of a person because he can't do what you can. Don't tell him he needs to get better. If he wants to, then help him, but don't tell him he has to.

- Listen to His Problems: The best thing you can ever do is just listen when he wants to talk. Not only will you learn some new things, but you will show him that you are invested in him, and by showing him a little compassion, you make him feel like he is important.

This scenario will show you how respect and compassion can help save a relationship.

Scenario

Rachel was worried about Rick. He had been acting distant lately, and was gone a lot. He always hid his phone and wouldn't let her touch it. Everyone said that he was probably cheating, but she trusted him to have a good reason for all of these things. She didn't want to be let down again by another man.

I will have a talk with him when he gets home tonight. I will ask him why he has been acting this way.

Suddenly she heard a phone ring. She checked her pockets, but it wasn't hers. She investigated the sound, and found her boyfriend's phone behind the toilet. There was a strange number calling.

Should I answer it? No. I trust him. It is probably just a telemarketer, and his phone probably fell behind the toilet this morning, and he didn't grab it cause he was running late to work.

Rachel knew that Rick would be home in a few hours, so she busied herself with errands and cleaning the house up. Five o'clock rolled by, and Rick still wasn't home. She started to get worried, and with no way to contact him, she couldn't allay her fears. But she told herself to remain calm, and that he would show up.

Finally, around seven o'clock, Rick came walking in the door. Rachel flung herself into his arms because she was so worried. Then she noticed that he didn't smell like the fiberglass mill, and he was surprisingly clean for being at work all day.

"Rick. We really need to talk." Rachel whispered, on the verge of tears.

"What's wrong?" Rick asked her

"I have been trusting of you, and I still trust you to tell me what is going on. I am trying not to assume you are cheating. However it is really hard to think of any other explanation why you have been coming home late, hiding your phone behind the toilet and getting strange calls. I didn't answer it by the way. Your clothes are too clean to be coming out of the fiberglass company, and they are the same clothes you walked out of here wearing. You don't smell like you normally do after work. Please just tell me what is going on." Rachel burst into tears.

"Oh Rach." Rick sighed, pulling her into his arms. "I got laid off a couple of weeks ago, and have been looking for a job ever since. That number was probably a job calling so I have to call back tomorrow. I'm late because I have been doing odd jobs to continue making enough money to support us, so you don't have to. I wanted to tell you, I just didn't want you to worry."

"That is what this is all about? You knew I was cheated on several times by my last guy, and you leave me worrying that it is happening again? Babe, I would have understood if you had told me, and I would have supported you, and even got a job myself if need be. I love you, and I want you to tell me about your problems. Please don't hide something like this again."

"Oh Rachel, I love you so much, and I didn't realize how bad it looked. I am so sorry, and I promise to always tell you about these things from now on." Rick said, kissing Rachel passionately.

Discussion

Rachel could have jumped to conclusions and accused Rick of cheating on her, thus making him angry for her not trusting him. However, she decided to ask him about it and listen to what he had to say. She was understanding when he told her what was going on, and let him know she wanted him to bring his troubles to her, even if it meant that he had to put some stress on her. She wanted to take on these problems together.

By being compassionate, and respecting him enough to trust him, she avoided what could have been a really big fight. Instead they were brought closer together, as they opened up with what was bothering them.

Why is this Key Important Again?

You have to respect each other to get anywhere in a relationship. Without respect you have nothing, and you can't truly love someone if you do not respect them. Compassion is needed to ensure that your relationship is not a miserable one. You have to respond with compassion to avoid having an argument blown out of proportion. People are not robots or dolls, they will mess up.

You have to use this key to unlock the part of a man's heart that trusts you. He doesn't open it up for just anyone. Most men do not trust half of the people they say are close to them. They could not be vulnerable to these people. You have to unlock that for yourself.

Chapter 5:

Secret Key #3

Be Confident

Men do not want to be with a woman who is always questioning if she is good enough for him. They want a woman who knows her worth. Men want to know they are with someone who feels valued. If you aren't confident, it makes his job of making you feel secure that much harder. He feels he always has to lift your self esteem, and that can be a hard job for anyone.

Confidence is not always just knowing you are worthy of love, however. It is also taking care of yourself. Taking care of your personal hygiene and keeping yourself groomed. You do not have to be perfect, just put an effort into keeping yourself clean and well kept.

Most people don't realize that this is important in a relationship, and that is what makes it a secret key. It is important to use this to unlock his desires for you if you are looking to start a relationship with him, and you must remain confident and well kept to unlock his never waning desires for you.

Confidence

Everyone has their insecurities, there is no doubt about that. However it is important to not let your insecurities rule your life. You can have some things that make you not so sure about yourself, but you have to be able to work through them.

Confidence is important in any aspect of your life, but it is certainly important in relationships. Not only do you have to be confident in yourself, you have to be confident in your relationship as well. You can't expect a relationship to thrive if you don't have any confidence in it. You have to believe that it will succeed, and that you are good enough for it to succeed.

In this scenario, you will learn more about what poor confidence can do to a relationship.

Scenario

Blake was super insecure. He constantly doubted himself, and if he was good enough for his boyfriend Michael. Michael hated that Blake was so insecure, and wished he could see how gorgeous he was. It caused many fights, because Blake felt that he wasn't good enough and did everything in his power to make Michael see that. Which included picking fights for no reason at all.

I wish I was confident enough to make this relationship work. I am just not good enough for him. He is perfect, and I am a fat lard. I really need to lose weight. I am so fat. Why does he stay with me? Can't he see I'm a disaster?

These are the thoughts that went through Blake's head daily. He couldn't ever get close to Michael, because he was scared that Michael would see that he was a disaster. He constantly had a wall up that Michael was trying to break down.

I'm exhausted. Blake never lets me in, and I'm am so tired of trying to break through the walls he puts up. I wish he could see how much he means to me. He is perfect just the way he is, if only he would stop worrying so much.

Michael was tired of always trying to boost Blake's self esteem, so with a heavy heart, he broke up with Blake.

"I told you I wasn't good enough!" Blake screamed, with tears in his eyes.

"You imbecile! That is the reason I am breaking up with you! You don't feel like you are good enough for me, and I am tired of you ignoring every effort I make to try to show you otherwise! You are perfect just the way you are, and I wish I could have made you see that! I don't want to leave, but I can't keep breaking my heart when you won't let me into yours!" Michael yelled back.

"So you aren't breaking up with me because I'm not breaking up with you, you are merely breaking up with me because I feel like I am not?" Blake whispered

"Yes. I want nothing more than to be with you, but I have to think of my own emotional health as well."

"What if I promised to get help for my insecurities? Would you stay with me? I love you Michael, I just don't want to be hurt anymore. I want you to love me too."

"I do love you Blake, and if you actively get help, then yes, I will stay. But you have two weeks to show me you are trying." Michael said, embracing Blake.

Discussion

Blake's insecurities almost cost him the love of his life. He was so worried about Michael pushing him away, that he didn't realize he was the one doing the pushing. Blake was not confident in himself, and it was tiresome for Michael to always be the one to supply the confidence for the both of them. Michael felt like Blake couldn't truly love him, because he never let him in. It almost destroyed their relationship beyond repair.

If Blake had realized that Michael wanted to be with him for who he was, he would have avoided this whole scene, and been very happy. Let your confidence shine through. You may not feel confident, but fake it until you make it. If you seem confident, you will start to feel confident.

Take Care of Yourself

Men want women to be healthy. This does not mean that you have to eat organic food, and wear full face makeup every day of your life. Just shower regularly, and keep yourself groomed. If you are a slob, and unhygienic, most men will feel that is a sign of lack of confidence, and they will stay away from you. You have to make yourself appear to be ready for a relationship to find the right relationship. If you look like you don't care about yourself you are going to attract someone who doesn't care about you as well.

If you are in a relationship, and start letting yourself go, you will make your man feel like you don't care about the relationship as much as you used to. (This doesn't count if you have kids. Though you should still try to shower regularly) You should always want to keep your hygiene up regardless of your relationship status.

Why is this Key Important?

This key unlocks a man's desire for you. Human's primal instinct is to mate, and men are really close to their primal instincts. He will be looking for a strong woman suitable for carrying his children, so that his offspring are strong and successful. By being confident, and taking care of yourself, you attract men that will value you, and treat you well. If you are not confident, and do not take care of yourself, you often will attract losers and abusers.

Chapter 6:

Secret Key #5

Give and Take on the Lead

This key is one of the most secret keys there are, because most people don't realize that the man doesn't always wear the pants in a relationship. You both have to make the big decisions together, and take turns on the smaller ones. You cannot let one single person take control of the relationship. If you work together, you unlock a bond that allows him to see you as an equal and not as below him.

If you make all of the decisions in the relationship, you allow him to be passive, but if he makes all the decisions, you become passive. Neither one of you should become passive, because this is a one way ticket to a controlling relationship. While it does not always end up that way, fifty six percent of relationships where one person is in charge of most or all of the decisions turn into be abusive relationships.

The solution to avoid this problem is to take turns making decisions. Even the smaller decisions like where to go when you go out to eat, or what to watch on television. On the bigger decisions, make them together. Especially on whether or not to buy a house or start a family, or any big purchase.

Also, take care of finances together, or split them up equally. You cannot give one person complete control of the finances, and expect to not have some control issues. Money is the biggest player in a controlling relationship. If one person has all the control of the money, they can tell the other partner what they can and cannot do, and once you get a taste of that power, it escalates from there.

The best way to avoid this is to get a joint account if you are married that has both of your names on it, so you both can access the funds, or have separate accounts with only your name on it, so the other partner can't access the funds. If you do this though, you have to decide how to split the bills. Otherwise, there will be issues with bills not getting paid, and utilities being shut off. This is if you live together. If not, you don't have to worry about it.

If you don't want to take turns on even the little decisions, then work together to decide everything. From where you want to eat, to where you want to live. Working together will create a strong bond between you two as well. You will grow closer together as you achieve things together. Think about it. If you make great strides in your life with the one you love, who are you going to celebrate with? That's right, them. So it only makes sense that if you make all your decisions together, you will grow closer due to the fact that you celebrate every achievement as one. You have to want to work together though, otherwise, you will argue more than you work together.

Why is this Key Important?

You want to unlock his heart in a way that makes him see you as an equal rather than a lesser, as society tries to make everyone think. If he sees you as his equal, he will learn to depend on you, rather than walk all over you. There will be less debates on who should make what decisions, and who is always right, because you will both be able to compromise and work together to achieve a blissful relationship.

PART III

Women are a puzzle for men to figure out. Just as women have to figure out men. Each person is a different puzzle and when you find the piece that fits, you have a long lasting relationship. Figuring out the secret to women or the woman you are currently in a relationship with—is easier than ever.

You have a guide that will help you think about the women you are typically interested in dating, currently dating or even married to. Just because you succeed in marrying a woman does not mean the work is over. Marriage is work. Any relationship takes work and involvement.

As a secret key, you cannot expect it to work with every woman you meet. Some women are simply unwilling to open their hearts. You will be given the tools to recognize when a woman is close-hearted, so you know that she is the wrong person for you.

The one thing you cannot forget as you read through this guide—is that you have to decide how much work you are willing to put into the relationship you wish to have. If you are reading this guide hoping you can unlock a woman's heart and then wish to become complacent, your relationship is doomed from the beginning.

Some women also take more work than others. They can have complicated lives or enjoy a little "too much" drama in how they act; therefore, you have to decide what you want in a relationship to gain a serious long term commitment.

You probably didn't think that you are part of the secret key. Yet, you are. Chemistry will only take you so far. A long term relationship, where the woman gives you her full heart begins with you.

So why do you need these "secret keys?" You need them because you want to unlock a woman's heart to its full potential. You want your relationship to go beyond the normal level because you want to be among the 10% who are blissfully happy. Only men who discover the secret of how a woman thinks, what she wants, and her ultimate desire to open her heart to the right man, will be among the elite happy couples in the world.

Discover the path to finally gain access to the "one's" heart that you wish to spend the rest of your life with, through the good and the bad.

CHAPTER 1

WHAT DO YOU WANT?

Do you walk into an electronics store or a car dealership without knowing what you want? No, if you are like most men, you buy magazines that tell you all the technical specs about the latest technology and cars. You also go online to forums and tech websites to do research.

Why would you try to pick up women or try dating sites without knowing what you want? You do not want to do that. If you are like most men, then you have dated, enjoyed one-night stands, and explored the pool of women.

Now, you are reading this book because you are looking for something more. Perhaps, you haven't dated more than a few women and wonder what you are doing wrong?

The men who are successful in relationships, who find those long term marriages—they are the ones who know what they want.

I'll give you an example of a marriage that lasted 42 years. It would have lasted longer if illness did not exist. This couple met when the wife moved into a new apartment complex with two other female friends. The young man, at the time, came up to see if there was anyone he wanted to date or would want to go on dates with him.

He would call up the night he wanted to date and see if someone was willing. He even spent eight months in another state. But, this man realized he had met the one person for him in that apartment.

He came back from living in a different place with one thing in mind—to ensure this woman would date him. He tried his nonchalant style, calling up the day of to ask for a date. She would always refuse because she also had other plans already in the works.

Finally, this man asked, "what do I have to do to get you to go out with me?"

The answer was simple, "call in advance."

The couple dated a few times before Christmas, every week during January and were engaged the day before Valentines.

Life doesn't always happen this way, but you can be sure that the man knew what he wanted. He dated several women, going out when they were available, and enjoying coffee, a meal, or a movie. But, no one caught his attention as much as the woman he married. It took distance to realize that no other woman compared.

If you have not dated very many people, then you need to get out there. You need to start dating more. How else are you supposed to figure out what you want?

I'll give you another example. This couple was together for 17 years and married for 13, almost 14 years. The marriage ended with a divorce and two suffering children. The man dated only two people, marrying the second. The woman had dated more men, but also enjoyed being the center of attention, the person that knows it all, and the person who lies because she doesn't recognize the truth. When the husband asked her father for her hand, the father said, "she is just like her mother, are you sure you know what you are doing?" Her mother constantly spends every dime that is earned, is all about herself, and often depressed and unhappy.

Of course, the husband thought he could live with it all, only to find that the woman he was marrying could easily ask for a divorce and immediately move in with another man.

The lesson in this second example is—you can know what you want and what you are capable of living with, but you also have to make allowances for the other person.

A person who cannot love themselves will never be able to love another with their whole heart.

Are you willing to accept being second or loved with less than a whole heart? Are you willing to date or marry someone when, you know, eventually, it will come to an end, it's just a matter of how long it takes?

These are the questions you need to ask yourself as you begin to learn the secrets to enter a woman's heart completely. Only when you know yourself and what you are willing to accept, can you truly find your way into the right woman's heart.

CHAPTER 2

SECRET KEY #1

Open, Honest, Consistent Communication

Pick up a woman's magazine that has a quiz. I bet that quiz has a section on communication. It probably tests the woman on how communicative her partner is and offers advice on how to elicit more communication. There are millions of these quizzes and articles in magazines, online, and they are all designed for woman by woman. Yet, you can learn something from this concept. Why do you think communication is such a hot topic? It is because women are fundamentally different from men.

Women can be extremely intuitive, even read body language, but women still consider the way men think a mystery. Women cannot believe a man is only thinking about sex. There has to be something more in your brains, right? You are capable of multitasking at your job, of dating multiple women, and holding deep conversations on politics, religion, engineering or something equally complicated—so you must have more on your mind than sex.

You also have feelings. These feelings can be hurt. You can also be excited and feel love. Women are unable to understand why you are unable to talk about these deeper feelings, and demand that you do.

A group of women get together and they catch up. What has happened in your life, what are you doing now, what happened last week. The conversation invariably turns to emotions, but it is not the whole discussion.

Women seek other women for emotional support and understanding because they feel they lack it from the men in their life. Women also work on hormones more so than men.

It's a fact and not something you should fear discussing. A woman can be happy one moment and the wrong words can flip a switch. The grudge can be held for days with the wrong words. A man usually forgets about the issue in a few hours or days, unless the same thing keeps happening.

So, on one hand, women have a need to know your emotions because they cannot understand them unless you tell them. On the other, there are emotional mind fields that you have to navigate as you communicate.

It has been the experience of most women that men do not want to communicate about their feelings. They find it a waste of time. Yet, it is the one thing that will help your woman feel confident in the relationship. It is the way for you to work your way into their heart.

The key is for this communication to be open, honest and consistent.

Defining Open

What does open communication mean? In business, it is a setting where employees are encouraged to share their thoughts and concerns, without the fear of retaliation (reference.com). In a relationship, it is the same thing, only the thoughts and concerns to be shared are about personal situations.

Communication includes issues about one's job, the treatment of the person by their boss, monetary concerns, kids, religion, love, and all other feelings people have.

For example, a family of four sat around a dinner table to discuss whether a move to a new state would be the best option for their family. The discussion included the changes that would occur, the employment options for the parents, and why the move would offer monetary stability versus the current place they lived. Each person was given a chance to discuss their thoughts, fears, concerns, and acceptance of the move.

Another family of four also moved. In this family, the parents sat their children down, said they were moving, and stated where. No communication from the children was allowed as to how they felt or why a move had to occur.

Do you think the children in the first family were more prepared and less unsettled than the second family? Of course, they were. They weighed in with their opinion, fears, concerns, and desires. The second family's children had to keep what they thought to themselves.

Now, consider this example, as a communication between two people: You have two people in a relationship, where one person is always stating what is going to happen, without giving reasons or why it is the best? How unsettled will the partner be? How angry do you think they will become at not having a choice?

Open communication is required to help your woman understand how you think, the reasons behind your actions, and to feel secure in the relationship. If you do not share your thoughts and feelings, how are they to know what you are really thinking? How are they to feel secure that you truly care about them, if they are not kept in the loop or considered part of the equation.

The game telephone provides a good example of this concept. One person starts a statement and by the end of ten or twenty people the statement has changed drastically. By the time your body signals based on your emotions are translated by a woman, they are changed because she is going to interpret them based on how she thinks, just like you try to interpret her behavior based on how you think.

Without communication, you are unable to figure out what each of you is thinking.

Honest Communication

Does this outfit make me look fat? Yes. Ouch. But, it is also how you deliver the answer. You need to be honest because there is one thing a woman does not want—she doesn't want to wear something that does not look good and she will feel embarrassed about later on. Also, here is the kicker—if you lie about how she looks in an outfit—what else could you be lying about?

It is far better to tell the truth when asked for it, then to lie. Furthermore, it is 100% better to speak the truth in any situation. If there is a behavior that bothers you, speak up. One woman told her husband this, "If I start acting like my mother, tell me." She was fearful that she would start displaying certain negative behavior that her mother had and she didn't want to. She was always hurt when being told "you are acting like your mother," but it also helped her realize that a correction to her behavior was required.

A woman who loves herself and gives of herself, completely, to the man she loves is capable of accepting the truth. The anger and stewing for a few hours is better than ignoring the problem or lying to avoid conflict.

Now will all women agree, no. Some women are unable to take the hurt that honest communication provides, but ask yourself, do you want a woman who can give her whole heart because she values your honesty or the woman who keeps a grudge and eventually causes too much pain?

You want the woman who can give her whole heart, so be honest in your communication and explain why you will always tell the truth, even if it is not what the person wants to hear. You'll be valued for this behavior because you are noticing and trying, as well as remaining truthful.

Consistency

More times than I have fingers I have seen relationships start where each person is honest, and communicative. However, after a year or two, the communication stops being consistent. It is like each man and woman believe they have figured the person out and know what they are thinking, so it is less necessary to be communicative.

Wrong.

You cannot become complacent just because it seems like the woman is not demanding communication as often as she was. There are only a few reasons she feels communication is no longer as necessary:

- She thinks she knows you well enough that she can read your moods.

- She is no longer interested.

- She is angry when you don't truly communicate.

If it is the first, then you need to show her that talking each night before you go to sleep is important to you. You need to give of yourself for her to continue giving of herself.

If she is no longer interested, you need to know, so you can move on to find the right person. Sometimes a woman has just as much difficulty breaking off a relationship. She doesn't want to cause hurt when she is unwilling to give her whole heart.

The last reason is fairly easy to discern. If you have not provided any worthwhile communication, then she will turn away, say "fine, whatever," or something along those words and stop trying to communicate with you.

For communication to unlock your woman's heart, you need to:

- Learn to read body language

- Read the subtle nuances in her tone

- And give of yourself before you ask her to give of herself

If you are embarrassed about your thoughts because they are just about "sex" in that moment—don't be. Tell her. But more than anything, have a time of day when the two of you talk about what happened at work, the challenges or the good things, and plans that you have or things that you want to do.

The conversation does not have to be deep and always about emotions each night. Rather, you are supposed to come together, be honest, be consistent, and just share. You are not to judge, just to listen, with attentiveness. If you only hear the words, then you cannot repeat them.

Here is something else that is usually a complaint from a guy, "all she has ever said are complaints. We never talk about anything other than how much she hates this or that."

Did you ever think that perhaps she is not happy with something that could be changed? Perhaps she needs a new perspective? Maybe, feelings of unhappiness in other areas of her life are making her complain about something else? The biggest one—did you ever think that she only communicates when there is something negative?

Try it, if you are already in a relationship. Track your communication for a week. Did your woman want to talk when she was happy or did she only want to talk when something was bothering her? Did you try to get her to talk about her day or the happy stuff, or did you think "yay, I don't have to try communicating today?"

Your effort to get her to talk when she is happy, will be rewarded. She will know that she can talk about anything, but more that you care to listen about everything. She will learn to talk about the good and the bad, so you don't hear only the unhappy things.

Thus, the ultimate secret is your effort in getting her to communicate about all things, just as much as she is asking you to communicate about anything at all.

One man said, "I didn't think you wanted to listen. I figured it would bore you."

His statement was definitely an insight into why he lacked communication. It was also the key his partner needed to understand that she needed to put more effort into listening.

Most try to say that communication is a two-way street, but is it really? If you drive on a two-way street, you have to keep to your own lane to avoid an accident. I suppose you could "meet in the middle," and block traffic. I'd rather think of communication as a one-way street. One of you has to be illegally driving to meet in the middle, but sometimes that is what it takes for a heart to open. If you are not willing to put in the effort to circumvent any blocks in the way, such as illegally driving down a one-way street, then how can you open up her heart?

She will see the motivation and honesty in your effort to communicate on all subjects that are important to you and her, not just what may be important to her. This will open her heart a little further, and allow her to trust in your feelings for her.

CHAPTER 3

SECRET KEY #2

Equality and Respect

This is a chapter that should be common sense, but more often than not, it is not. Countries were founded on inequality and there are many still struggling with inequality issues to the point that women are killed if they step out of line. Given how sensitive a topic this is—it should not surprise you that all women want to be treated equally and with respect.

Yes, there are people with more intellect than others, but talking down to them or disrespecting them is not the proper way to communicate. What if you were faced with a woman who had an IQ of 185 and she consistently talked down to you even about simple topics? A man's pride gets pricked pretty easy. It is annoying when a woman is or acts smarter than you. So, why wouldn't it be annoying and insensitive if you are always acting smarter than the woman you are with.

Here is an example: A young man not very well versed in subtle body language and common sense would talk about simple things, a topic that he had in common with a young woman. But, he would often use an arrogant tone with an

"I know more than you" attitude. He would tell this young woman things she already knew, like she didn't know the first thing about it.

The relationship didn't last. Nor will any relationship in this situation, when the woman is capable of knowing herself, her own intellect, and a proper way of having a conversation.

It doesn't have to always be about conversation, either. It is just an easy example that helps shore up the previous chapter.

When you communicate in a relationship, the woman wants to be seen as your equal, to have an equal opinion. She doesn't want her words discounted because you know better.

She wants her words to resonate, for you to think about them, and help explain why something else would be better or why her opinion is valued, but not the right approach.

For example, let's say you are married and you have a child. Your child starts to refuse to eat. You might have a different viewpoint than your wife. Your wife might allow the child to go to bed without food until the child finally figures out that starving is not the answer. You might not want your child to go to bed hungry, so you will allow your child to choose a healthy snack such as apples and cheese.

Your wife feels that you are giving in to your child and their refusal to eat healthy things. You might feel that letting your child go hungry, can have unhealthy consequences. Who is right or wrong? That is not the answer. The question is who is going to see results quicker? If the father will get the child to eat healthy foods, then the child will remain healthy. If the child continues to not eat enough, even with healthy snacks then this can hinder the path to a solution. Whereas, starving often gets a child to eat, even a little of something they don't like or a willingness to try it cooked a different way in order to never go to bed hungry again.

The debate won't be answered here because the point is not to solve the question, but to realize that if you refuse to listen to your partner's opinion, harm could be done in more ways than one. You could end up hurting your child and on the other hand, you are putting your wife in a position of disrespect in front of the child.

Dismissing what your partner, whether you are dating, going to the next step, or married, is not going to get her to open her heart to you. Are you always right 100% of the time in all areas? Of course not, and neither is your partner.

The key is for you two to be able to see each other as equals. You look at each other, know your strengths and weaknesses, and compromise when necessary, but never with a disrespectful attitude.

It is okay to point out certain mistakes, but make sure you do it with respect. Value the person and they will open their heart to you. They will also value you more, for showing that you value them.

If you have not yet noticed this is leading to "trust." For a woman to give their entire heart to you—they need to trust you, trust that you understand them, respect them, and value what they have to say or to give in the relationship.

Communication is not the only way to make this known. Body language is also very important in a woman being seen as an equal. If you ignore something they say or do, it is an act of disrespect, of seeing them as less.

For you it may be complacency. You might be used to the person always cooking your dinner, so you forget to say thank you or take notice of their hard work. The husband or boyfriend who is successful never lets anything go unnoticed.

Car Doors and Other Doors

"She has her own hands; she can open the door."

Have you ever thought this? Perhaps you know someone who has? Maybe, the women you have dated told you it is unnecessary to open doors for her?

Yes, a woman likes to do for herself, but that doesn't mean you should never open a door for her. Choose your moments. Make it a surprise. Even a woman who is capable and willing to open her own doors, appreciates when a gentleman will do it for her. It is based on when you open the door.

For instance, let's say your girlfriend has her arms full of things and there is no hand to open the door. You would immediately open it for her, right? Of course.

The next time you need to open the door is when you are taking her out for a special dinner.

"Let me get the door." This statement tells her that you appreciate that she is coming with you and that she has dressed lovely for the evening. It is a "special" occasion that supersedes the usual rule that she will open her own doors.

If you are running late and it is easier for your partner to open her door, then wait and she doesn't mind opening her own door—it is okay to let her. If she is the type that always needs the door open as a sign of chivalry, then you still, have to open it.

It is not about the door. It is about the effort and respect such an action provides. Again, you let the woman make a choice based on her preferences or you simply ask what she prefers. You choose your moments to be sweet or you always show respect because that is what your heart tells you to do.

There are men who will tell a woman, "I was raised to open doors as a sign of respect. Not complying with this, goes against the respect I have for you."

The key again is to communicate what you know to be right, so that your partner also understands your point of view.

You should back down to show your respect, but also in the same light tell her that you are respecting her more by following through with certain instincts.

Remember these suggestions are examples. You have your upbringing and your partner will have hers. As long as you show mutual respect for each other, and equality of the minds, then you will have a woman who is willing to show you her heart.

CHAPTER 4

SECRET KEY #3

Acceptance for Who They Are

What is the one thing many women have tried to do when they started dating you? They tried to change you. The wrong woman always tries to change her partner. They want you to fit into an ideal they have for a man. There are plenty of reasons for this.

- She is afraid of never finding someone who will accept her

- She feels you are broken and in need of fixing

The two bullet points are the two main reasons she may try to change you. A smart woman will eventually realize that she cannot change the man she is dating. She has to accept him for who he is, his faults and strengths, or find someone else.

You may wish to change the woman you are dating too. Perhaps she doesn't care enough about her appearance? Maybe, she shops and spends too much money? It may be something simple that you do not like, but cannot seem to ignore.

You have an option. You can stop dating a person because she has habits or traits you cannot ignore or you can accept them. It is your choice, but you need to make it.

Don't stay with someone because of your own fear. Yes, men do have fears. There are men out there who fear that they will have to settle for one woman because the one they want is unattainable. Did you ever think that you are not settling, but finding the person who is right for you? Do not settle if things do not feel right and in the same vain do not choose a woman who you cannot accept for her faults and strengths.

If you already have problems or fights due to basic personality clashes, then you are not going to get the woman to stay with you and give her full heart.

The secret is to truly accept, no matter what or to realize that you cannot. If you can accept all of her faults, then you will open her heart a little more, and eventually her whole heart will be yours.

The one thing you cannot do is change your mind and expect her to open her heart. She has to know that there is consistency within your own heart.

You either accept her for who she is or you don't. If you do not really accept her faults, then you will always have doubts in your mind. You will always question or find yourself focusing on the things you cannot accept.

People can only change themselves if they see a problem. They are not going to change because you want the change to happen. For a time, they may try to be better, but after a while, their inherent traits will win out. There is no way around the traits winning, unless the person they are a part of is willing to change.

Yes, you received an example earlier that stated the wife wanted to know when she was acting like her mother. The key here is that she wanted to know. She asked for the truth. She was already in the frame of mind that she may need to change her behavior if she became like her mother.

If you try to point out things to a woman who has not asked or does not think there is something wrong within herself, then you are not going to succeed. She will close her heart and doubt that you can love her fully when you cannot accept all of who she is.

There is also a difference in accepting who a woman is and being her support for the changes that she wishes to make.

What if the woman you are dating had a bad family experience as a child? What if she lacks confidence? Can you deal with her frame of mind and self-doubt? What if you could be her support to help her build her self-confidence without actually pointing out that she needs the help?

It is possible. If you are open and willing to accept the woman for who she is and the potential of who she desires to be, then you are going to find her whole heart is in your hands.

By now you should see a theme in the secrets to a woman's heart: trust and support.

Any woman you date needs to feel they can trust you and that you will be supportive. Without trust and support, she is going to feel like you are only partially in the relationship and she is going to hold back.

It does not matter how many relationships you have had that reach the next level from dating casually to steadily. It does not matter if you have married before and your marriage has failed or is struggling. If you can provide trust and support for the woman you value in your life, you will finally succeed in opening her complete heart to you.

The Pedestal

One man succeeded and another did not. There was a time when one woman was dating two men. She would go out on Fridays with one guy and Saturdays with the other. Both men knew she was dating someone else, but they had never met. One man asked for her hand and was given a "yes." The other took her to a wrestling match the day she received the marriage proposal. The next date he found out she was going to marry the other guy and asked, "are you sure. I love you, you are everything to me, I've put you on a pedestal and don't know how I can live without you being my wife."

The woman's answer: "Your first mistake was putting me on a pedestal."

No one wants to be on a pedestal.

Already it was mentioned that you need to accept the woman for who she is. A part of this discussion is about that very concept. You do need to accept a woman's faults.

More importantly, you cannot raise a woman too higher than she truly is. You cannot have a "celebrity" image of the woman you wish to date.

What if every woman went around trying to find her perfect guy from the romance novels she reads or the songs that have been sung?

You know she won't find this guy because you know men have faults and are not romantic heroes like in the books and movies.

You cannot put a woman on a pedestal and expect a life of happiness to follow.

The minute you put a woman on a pedestal is the minute your relationship is wrong.

You have to be supportive and help her learn to trust you, but you cannot make her a "goddess," in your mind.

Do not keep the rose colored glasses on and reference what you truly want.

What do you wish to see in a woman you can spend your life with? Are you the type of man who needs space, but will never stray? Can you look at attractive women, but know that the one beside you, is the most attractive because of the entire package? If so, then you don't need a pedestal for her. You just need to marry her if you haven't already.

CHAPTER 5

SECRET KEY #4

The Pedestal

One man succeeded and another did not. There was a time when one woman was dating two men. She would go out on Fridays with one guy and Saturdays with the other. Both men knew she was dating someone else, but they had never met. One man asked for her hand and was given a "yes." The other took her to a wrestling match the day she received the marriage proposal. The next date he found out she was going to marry the other guy and asked, "are you sure. I love you, you are everything to me, I've put you on a pedestal and don't know how I can live without you being my wife."

The woman's answer: "Your first mistake was putting me on a pedestal."

No one wants to be on a pedestal.

Already it was mentioned that you need to accept the woman for who she is. A part of this discussion is about that very concept. You do need to accept a woman's faults.

More importantly, you cannot raise a woman too higher than she truly is. You cannot have a "celebrity" image of the woman you wish to date.

What if every woman went around trying to find her perfect guy from the romance novels she reads or the songs that have been sung?

You know she won't find this guy because you know men have faults and are not romantic heroes like in the books and movies.

You cannot put a woman on a pedestal and expect a life of happiness to follow.

The minute you put a woman on a pedestal is the minute your relationship is wrong.

You have to be supportive and help her learn to trust you, but you cannot make her a "goddess," in your mind.

Do not keep the rose colored glasses on and reference what you truly want.

What do you wish to see in a woman you can spend your life with? Are you the type of man who needs space, but will never stray? Can you look at attractive women, but know that the one beside you, is the most attractive because of the entire package? If so, then you don't need a pedestal for her. You just need to marry her if you haven't already.

CHAPTER 6

SECRET KEY #5

Make Her Smile

The key to most women's hearts is to make her smile and laugh. The right woman will accept your personality, whether it is sarcastic humor or witty humor. It is also the effort you provide in making her smile or laugh. For example, a coworker recently knew his female coworker was having a bad day. They are friends and nothing more, as there is a significant difference in age. Yet, the man, going through his own trials, still worked for a good hour to make her laugh and smile rather than to continue crying as she was doing.

This is a man who understands that humor, even in making silly faces, giving out zinger, witty remarks, is the key to making a woman fall a little in love, even if it is only friendship.

You don't have to be the wittiest. You may have a stupid joke that makes one groan more than laugh or smile. However, the effort in trying to make the woman smile, to make her laugh, will instantly make her heart melt.

Gifts are Important

Surprise gifts are important to a woman. They consider these gifts as supportive or endearing because you are paying attention to her. There are times when life gets routine, mundane, and even filled with complacency on both of your sides. The trick is to come home with a surprise.

Flowers are nice for some women. For others, they are an instant allergy issue. Some men feel that flowers are going to die, so why spend the money, when something else can be provided, such as a vacation from saving money on the little things.

The key is to know what your woman believes and what you can do that will matter to her heart. Sometimes it can be the silliest thing or the simplest. What if you both love tattoos? Did you ever think about getting a tattoo of a symbol or date that matters to both of you?

Perhaps, it is as simple as coming home with a card. Maybe when she goes on a business trip you hide a card in her bag moments before you say goodbye at the airport.

Gifts do not have to be expensive, they do not have to be jewelry, but they do need to be thought of and given. Yes, some women prefer expensive gifts, even demand them, and if you have a wife or partner like this, then you need to comply sometimes. It goes back to accepting and knowing the woman you have in your life. However, it doesn't mean that small things like cards and spontaneous gifts that are not expensive won't move her heart.

It is all about what you know about her desires, what she is used to, and what will make her smile and love you because of the effort you have shown. You can also show a woman used to expensive gifts that it is not the money, but the honesty behind the gift that matters the most.

CHAPTER 7

Special Bonus Tips

Not all women will fit your personality. There are some women who should not be in relationships or marry, unless they can find a partner who is just like them in the key ways. There are even some women who will never open their heart and find true happiness because they cannot find it in themselves. These bonus tips will help you look at relationships and women, so you might succeed, when you have faced certain issues such as being in a bad relationship, failing to be supportive in small ways, or even noticing her each and every day.

Things to Look Out For

- Does your current partner feel love is shown through how much you buy her?

- Does she flirt with other men to see if you are getting angry or noticing what she is doing?

- Does she seem to pick a fight or get angry for no reason you can see?

- Has she started to withdraw from you?

- Is she starting to ignore you, your phone calls, or breaking dates?

These are a few signs that you need to look out for in understanding that she is not the woman for you. Some of these can also be a sign that she may have a psychological issue that she cannot get passed and will eventually affect the relationship.

For instance, have you ever date a woman who lies, who tries to separate you from friends and family, needs "things" to feel you love her, and is always thinking about herself? This can be the sign of a narcissist. A narcissist is someone who views themselves as the most important, cannot handle when someone else is more important, is often arrogant, and knows everything. This same person also blames everyone around them for being at fault and for doing things they are actually doing.

Toxic relationships like this need to be avoided, even if you feel you can live with this person's faults. Drama is another word that has been applied to women who seem to cause conflict, always pick a fight, and have a healthy sexual appetite that never seems satisfied with just one person.

Only you can truly say what type of relationship you are looking for, but there are definitely signs that you need to watch out for with regards to women and drama they can create.

- A woman can call you several times a day or demand that you call them often.

- They may ask where you were and not trust your answer.

- They may text or try to start up a conversation that is too deep on the first meeting.

- They may complain and find nothing happy.

These are just a few other signs that a woman may not be right for you or perhaps anyone. Someone who is obsessive without actually dating you can have psychological issues that require a professional. It may not be nice to say of one's own sex, but it is also the truth. Some women need to recognize their failings and accept those in order to find a healthy relationship, otherwise they are "crazy" in their actions towards men, bordering on obsessive.

Signs of a Wrong Relationship

Relationships do not have to be filled with "crazy" or drama to be wrong for you. There are definite signs that a woman is not right for you, when she is unwilling to give her heart to you. It is not a matter of you trying harder to be supportive, and not complacent in the relationship.

Here is an example of a woman. See if you can see why she might be wrong for a relationship with you.

- She prefers her own company to others.

- She has social anxiety.

- She needs a routine and does not like that routine to be interrupted.

- She is hyper-organized, hating when someone fills up a space she just cleaned.

- She cannot trust easily.

- She is unwilling to be hurt and face the loss of a husband, preferring to die before any of her family, so she doesn't have to face that horrible situation.

- She also has a dislike of touch, something no one can pinpoint a cause for, but one that holds her from a deep physical relationship.

Obviously, this is an extreme example, but take note of it. Sometimes the signs are subtle and other times there is a big sign saying "this is not right." A woman who does not allow physical contact after three dates either has issues with physical contact or does not see you as a sexual partner. A relationship that is not right for you will have fights, ups and downs, and disagreements on the main issues. You won't be able to agree on politics, religion, children, and life in general.

Additional Effort Options

A couple was having trouble in their marriage. The wife was unhappy.

The man knew it, but couldn't figure out what to do. He decided he would ask her each morning, "what can I do to make your day better?" At first, his wife thought he was being insensitive and joking. After he kept asking she realized that he meant it and started answering, as well as asking how she could make his day better.

Such a simple phrase and the care behind it saved the marriage. You can do something like this in your relationship. It doesn't have to be a big deal. It can be something as simple as asking how your partner's day was or how you can make it better.

It can also be something that will make her smile. The married couple of 42 years is another great example. One child was grown, married, and nearing having children. The second child left home to live 3,000 miles away. Living as just the two of them, the wife was missing her children. To make her day better, the husband took one of the stuffed animals his daughter left when she moved away, and started creating funny scenes.

One day the orangutan stuffed animal was holding a fake cigarette and reading in their bed. The next day it was playing chess with one of the wife's stuffed bears of similar size. For over a week, the husband would wake up, create a scene, leave for work, and his wife would come home to it. She would smile. Now she has pictures of these scenes to help her memory, since the husband passed away from early onset dementia.

These little efforts changed the wife's outlook for the day, the ache in her heart from missing her daughter, and now is a comfort to her with him gone.

What can you think to do that would have such a lasting impact because it is guaranteed to open the woman's heart for life.

Flowers are acceptable, of course, and even desired by most women. But, if you have the imagination, find something that can truly make her smile, laugh, or even cry with happiness. It matters.

Helping Your Partner become a Better Her

The couple who spent 42 years together respected each other, loved each other, and were best friends as well as husband and wife. One of the biggest impacts the husband had on his wife, was mutual respect, equality, and the power to give her what made her a better version of herself. This is not about changing the person, but giving her the tools to go after what she desires.

The wife was told by her mother on more than one occasion that she was stupid, worthless and that her mother wished she had never been born. Her only choice of work was to go to a trade school. Given the year she graduated, her only real choice was to become a hairdresser. It was not something she hated, but her husband also gave her the choice of being able to do more and spend more time with her children as they grew.

In fact, she started working with her husband on construction sites building houses as a family. It gave her more freedom to spend with her children, as well as spend every day with her husband. When she would ask can "I do this or do that," such as take ballet, he told her "you never have to ask. You can do what you want to do."

He gave her the power to try different things and be who she was, without judgement. It helped that they had the money for her to try new things, but all the same he told her they were equal that the money they made was hers to spend as she wished.

Now, she was also brought up in a poor family, so spending money was a difficult decision. She never spent money that was earmarked for bills, groceries, and necessary monthly expenses. She was responsible in the spending, but also given the chance to explore and do.

It made her heart open more for this husband. You may find that you are drawn to such a woman yourself. You also need to realize that while she is becoming a better version of herself because of you, she can also make you a better version of yourself. It is not about changing who you are inherently, but about taking what you are, loving who you are, and helping you be the best you can be even in the face of adversity.

The person who can allow this and accept such help in return is the person that can form a long term, lasting relationship with the right woman. It is also the person who will have the whole heart of the woman he loves.

Withholding Due to Fear

A lack of support and trust in a relationship can lead to the woman you are dating or married to, fearing to give her whole heart to you. There are subtle signs you need to look for if the woman fears giving her heart.

- She will withhold herself too.

- She will often go on trips without you for business or to visit family, and not call.

- She will test to see if she can live without you.

- She will test you in communication to be more open in conversation.

- She will become angry or distant if you answer wrong or continue to withhold.

- More fights will occur.

- She will start to ask where you see the relationship going.

These are fear tests that she is giving you. She is hoping that you will realize her fear and start to open up, start to pay attention, and show her through action not words, how much she means to you.

If she is not the right woman, then don't let her live in fear. If she is the woman you wish to gain her whole heart, recognize the fear, address it, and start changing how you communicate, offer her your trust, and support.

What do you do if a woman says she is moving out? Do you let her or do you ask her what is going on?

If you have established open communication, where she feels she can trust you, but is not receiving proper support or respect, she will tell you her fear. If you have done nothing to gain her trust, respect, support, or communication she will be evasive and tell you "it's just not working or it's me not you."

For the right woman, you will strive to correct yourself to make her more comfortable and recognize your fault and the fear of the relationship she is feeling. If you cannot give her that, then you need to allow the relationship to end, learn from it, and start looking for the woman who is right for you.

Are you Clinging

There are certain turn offs for a woman.

- She does not want to be your mother.

- She does not want to constantly clean up after you.

- She does not want to cook you every meal you eat.

- She wants you to make an effort.

- She does not want you to call 10 times a day.

- She wants you to respect what she says and remember what she says.

- If she tells you no, then it is no. Not maybe, not flirting, not suggestive.

- If she asks for your opinion or a decision on what you want to do—give her one.

- A woman wants a decisive man, who knows himself, and is not afraid to laugh at himself.

Above all she does not want a man who clings. She does not want someone who is obtuse to her feelings or the subtle information she is giving him. She wants someone who is willing to pay attention, to be supportive, who will try to gain her trust, and love her so she can open her heart to him.

CONCLUSION

The secret to breakthrough with women are simple — create a situation where you are supportive and gain her trust. To be the one, you have to give of yourself before you ask her to give you all of herself.

Each woman is different in personality, tastes, and needs, but they are also fundamentally the same in needing to be important, respected, equal in mind and body, and loved unconditionally.

Only when you can be yourself, honest, supportive, and respect her fully can you be "the one" for her.

You also have to realize that sometimes a woman is unwilling to open her heart. Sometimes she may not see you as the one or no matter what you do to try opening her heart, she simply cannot.

If you can recognize that she is never going to open her heart to you, then you can move on to a woman who is willing.

Sometimes you definitely get lucky and met the "one" for you and marry three months later. Sometimes it takes years. You have to be open. You have to be willing. You cannot be complacent. You also have to know what you are looking for to recognize her when she comes along.

If you don't know your own mind, then you won't be able to see the woman who is right for you. She could be next to you, waiting for you to see her and waiting to open her heart to you. She may be the next woman you meet through an online dating service.

Only when you have the secret key to making sure you are supportive and giving her a reason to trust you—will you succeed.

You can do this. You now have insight into a woman's mind, examples of success and non-success. Now, take what you have learned and apply it to you and your unique situation or woman.

www.ingramcontent.com/pod-product-compliance
Lightning Source LLC
LaVergne TN
LVHW021232080526
838199LV00088B/4324